To Neil,

Thank you for helping this great
Country to realise another of their
amazing dreams.

Best wishes

David Neild

Qasr al Sarab 18·5·2017.

A Soldier
in Arabia

A Soldier in Arabia
David Neild

Published by
Medina Publishing Ltd
310 Ewell Road
Surbiton
Surrey KT6 7AL
medinapublishing.com
uae@medinapublishing.com

ISBN: 978-1-909339-63-7

Designed by Kitty Carruthers
Printed and bound by Emirates Printing Press llc, Dubai

CIP Data: A catalogue record for this book is available from the British Library.

A Soldier in Arabia

David Neild

Medina Publishing

Dedication

This book is dedicated to the long life of His Highness Sheikh Saqr bin Mohammed Al Qasimi, a truly great man. Throughout his 62-year reign, Sheikh Saqr worked tirelessly to improve the lives and conditions of his people and laid the foundations that have enabled Ras Al Khaimah to be transformed from a small coastal fishing region into the emirate it is today.

It is also dedicated to his son, HH Sheikh Saud bin Saqr Al Qasimi, the present Ruler of Ras Al Khaimah. Sheikh Saud has continued to build on his father's legacy with passion and skill and, as a result, business and tourism flourish in the scenic and tranquil environment of Ras Al Khaimah.

A Soldier in Arabia was also written to remember the officers and men with whom I was privileged to serve in the Trucial Oman Scouts, the Ras Al Khaimah Mobile Force and the Sharjah National Guard. I salute you all.

David Neild with HH Sheikh Saud bin Saqr Al Qasimi, Ruler of Ras Al Khaimah.

CONTENTS

HH Sheikh Saqr bin Mohammed
Al Qasimi, Ruler of Ras Al Khaimah
1948–2010

HH Sheikh Saud bin Saqr Al Qasimi,
Ruler of Ras Al Khaimah

FOREWORD

by
HH Sheikh Saud bin Saqr Al Qasimi
Ruler of Ras Al Khaimah

Our history shapes us profoundly. Our experiences and outlook on life are deeply influenced by the decisions and actions of those who have gone before us. We must know our history accurately if we are to build wisely on the work of our predecessors rather than be trapped by it.

David Neild first came to this region when many of the building blocks were being laid that would result in the formation of the UAE. He served here as an officer in the Trucial Oman Scouts on two separate tours and went on to establish the Ras Al Khaimah Mobile Force and, shortly afterwards, the Sharjah National Guard. His commitment, loyalty and professional military expertise earned the trust and respect of many including my father, His Highness Sheikh Saqr bin Mohammed Al Qasimi.

In this book he combines his eye-witness accounts of key events with careful research which places his experiences in their historical context.

By his military service David left a valuable legacy at the foundation of the UAE. By writing this book he has added to that legacy by leaving a record that will illuminate that period for generations to come.

Saud bin Saqr Al Qasimi

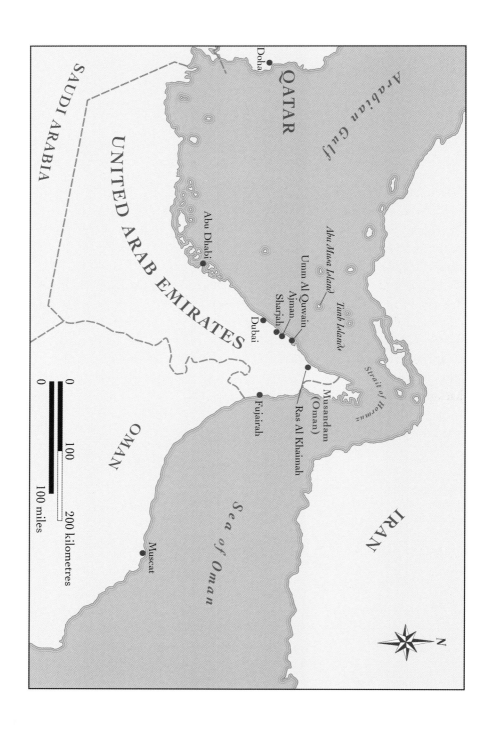

PREFACE

For many years my family and friends have encouraged me to write about my time in the Trucial States, which would enable me to recall the memorable personalities with whom I came into close contact and to describe some of the major historical events I was privileged to witness at first hand. I knew that the day would eventually come when I would be ready to sit down and begin these memoirs. It was simply a question of when.

In 2012, during an audience with HH Sheikh Saud bin Saqr Al Qasimi, the Ruler of Ras Al Khaimah, he asked me to write about my early military days in the region. He stressed that it should be a personal account, 'through my eyes', but should also include relevant background details of important events that had taken place in the region prior to the formation of the United Arab Emirates. I have known Sheikh Saud since he was a young man and am well aware of his strong desire to record the history and development of Ras Al Khaimah and the background to the creation of the United Arab Emirates. Having received this request from His Highness, I knew the time had finally come to relive the past and put my rusty memory to the test.

David Neild
Ras Al Khaimah, July 2015

HH Sheikh Saqr bin Mohammed Al Qasimi, Ruler of Ras Al Khaimah, with Lt Col David Neild, Commander of the Ras Al Khaimah Mobile Force, in 1971.

INTRODUCTION

The part of the Arabian Peninsula now called the United Arab Emirates has a fascinating history and, I believe, an exciting future. I am fortunate to have known the region since 1959, long before the formation of the UAE. This was a remarkable event when, just after Bahrain and Qatar became independent states, seven of the remaining independent states united to become one country. Under this arrangement Abu Dhabi, Dubai, Sharjah, Ajman, Fujairah, Umm Al Quwain and Ras Al Khaimah joined to form the United Arab Emirates, while each maintained its own individual character.

Ras Al Khaimah is the northernmost of the seven emirates that make up the UAE and the one I am now fortunate to call my home. Its history is closely linked to its maritime past. In the 1430s, Ahmed bin Majid was born in what was then known as Julfar. He became a famous maritime navigator and earned the nickname 'Lion of the sea'. Some historians credit him with piloting Vasco da Gama across the Indian Ocean from the east coast of Africa to India in 1497, although this is unlikely. Ibn Majid is still revered by Muslim mariners, and the Victorian explorer Sir Richard Burton recorded that, on sailing out of Aden in the mid-1800s, the sailors on board prayed in his honour. During his lifetime, Ibn Majid wrote more than 40 manuscripts, not only on navigation but also poetry, and two of his handwritten works are on display at the Bibliothèque nationale in Paris.

The Qawasim are the historical rulers of both Sharjah and Ras Al Khaimah, and trace their family history back to the Prophet Muhammad. The name probably originates from a Sheikh Qasim, the grandfather of Sheikh Rashid bin Mattar, who was Ruler of Sharjah and Ras Al Khaimah between 1760 and 1777, and the first family member to be mentioned in British records. The Qawasim were part of the Hawala tribe and lived for many centuries on both sides of the Gulf, including Lingeh and Qishm, now part of modern-day Iran. Sharjah and Ras Al Khaimah were important coastal trading towns long before Abu Dhabi and Dubai, which were then small, isolated fishing villages.

After establishing the East India Company in 1600 to capitalise on the lucrative trade between India and Europe, the British became increasingly sensitive to any interference with their trade. Towards the end of the 18th century, the British became more aggressive in 'protecting' their trade, restricting the activities of their competitors. They even went as far as requiring all ships trading in the Gulf to hold British 'passes'. Naturally, the local Arabs took exception to this interference in the trade on which they depended for their livelihoods.

It shows how dominant the Qawasim were at that time that the British referred to all the Arab tribes involved in these attacks as 'Joasmees', which is derived from the Qawasim name. These Joasmees were held responsible for numerous maritime acts of aggression, which commenced on 18 May 1797 with the capture of a British trading ship, *Bassein Snow*, which was released two days later. A far more serious incident took place in October 1797, when a 14-gun cruiser, HMS *Viper*, was attacked. Prior to the attack, the Qawasim Sheikh Salih had requested and received balls and powder from the commander of the British ship. The next morning, the *Viper's* captain went ashore and, while the crew were eating breakfast, Sheikh Salih fired on the ship, killing a Lieutenant Carruthers.

There followed a tranquil period at sea, but on land the Qawasim and the Sultan of Oman were engaged in constant tribal conflict. Occasional peace treaties would be agreed but these never lasted long before fighting broke out again. All this changed with the arrival, in 1800, of the Wahhabis from Saudi Arabia in the area known as the Buraimi Oasis. Initially the Omanis and Qawasim united to fight off this invasion but, by 1802, the whole region had been won over to the Wahhabis and their more fundamentalist way of life. Some historians believe it was the influence of the Wahhabis that triggered the revival of attacks by the Qawasim. In 1805, two English trading vessels were attacked: the *Shannon*, followed by the *Trimmer*. A treaty between the British and the Omanis to subdue the Qawasim activities and deter French ambitions collapsed in 1808. The Qawasim were then accused of being responsible for the attack on an eight-gun British schooner, HMS *Sylph*, which resulted in the slaughter of its Indian crew.

In May 1809 another British ship, HMS *Minerva*, was seized, taken to Ras Al Khaimah and held for ransom. On board this ship was a Mrs Taylor, the wife of one of the officers. Reports in the British press suggested that she had been paraded through the town and sold into slavery at a public auction. Fortunately, these salacious allegations proved false and, once a ransom had been paid for her release, she emerged from her ordeal unharmed and in good health.

Although the details from official records of the time are unclear, it is probable that the Supreme (British) Government in Calcutta had already taken the decision to punish the Qawasim even prior to the *Minerva* incident. A fleet of 16 ships, with a military force of several thousand British and Indian troops, set sail with an attack force jointly commanded by Captain Wainwright, captain of HMS *Chiffone*, and Lt Colonel Smith of the 65th Regiment.

After bombarding the area for two days, this large contingent went ashore on the coast of Ras Al Khaimah on 13 November 1809. They were met with fierce resistance as they waded chest-high to reach the shore before finally securing the beaches. The bravery of the Qawasim was no match for the superior military strength and weapons of the invaders and, after a battle lasting many hours, the British finally forced their way into the town. They then proceeded to set fire indiscriminately to the buildings and destroyed over 100 ships.

To prevent the Qawasim from rebuilding their fleet, the British imposed an embargo against the import of Indian teak, but this did not deter them. Within three years they had managed to rebuild the fleet, mainly with African wood, and by 1812 the Qawasim of Ras Al Khaimah were once more a powerful maritime force. But it was not long before they were again in dispute with the British.

The Qawasim resumed attacks, mainly on vessels sailing under the British flag, but frequently on Omani and even American and French ships as well, and expanded their maritime operations as far away as Bahrain. The Qawasim, who were by far the most dominant tribe in the region at the time, argued that no foreign power had the right to control their coastal waters or to curtail legitimate trade by their own ships. They complained bitterly that restricting the free passage of their vessels caused serious hardship for the coastal people and insisted that they were justified in their actions against foreign ships. This opinion was not shared by the British and ultimately the Governor of Bombay, Sir Evan Nepean, after consultation with Governor General Lord Hastings, agreed that decisive action was needed. An expedition force was then assembled, with the aim of suppressing the Qawasim and ensuring that they would never be a maritime threat again.

In December 1819, a British force, commanded by Major General Sir William Grant Keir, returned to Ras Al Khaimah. Its orders were to destroy all vessels and stores that had been used by the Qawasim in these attacks. By 9 December, after several days of heavy bombardment, the British fought their way inland. The spirited defence by the Qawasim was commanded by Hassan bin Rahman, who had become the principal sheikh in the area after the arrival of the Wahhabis.

The British force eventually entered all the coastal towns in the Ras Al Khaimah area, destroying every building and inflicting heavy casualties. This brutal assault left the Qawasim with little negotiating power and enabled the British to draft a permanent treaty to their advantage.

The treaty was drawn up by an interesting individual named Captain Perronet Thompson. He was the only Arabist included in the invading forces and was accompanied by his wife Anne and young son Charles on board the East India Company cruiser *Orient*. By March 1820, he had managed to obtain the signatures of the local tribal sheikhs of Abu Dhabi, Ajman, Dubai, Sharjah, Umm Al Quwain and Bahrain, as well as Ras Al Khaimah. The lengthy terms and conditions laid out in the 1820 treaty were actually drafted by Captain Thompson's wife. She wrote to her brother that 'all the copies of the Treaty signed, sealed and delivered to the various chiefs were in my handwriting'. (She also pointed out that she received no payment for her secretarial duties.) The rulers, even though some of them had not participated in any attacks on British ships had no choice but to agree to the many new restrictions, such as the prohibition of any involvement in slavery. It was also agreed that a garrison force of approximately 800 Indian soldiers and an artillery unit would remain in Ras Al Khaimah after the departure of the main force. Captain Thompson was placed in command of this garrison which, mainly due to the heavy loss of life caused by sickness and disease, remained for only a few months. The conditions to which the British forces were exposed were described in another letter from Anne Thompson. She wrote:

> The atmosphere seemed absolutely on fire, there was no air to breathe, and I was burning with fever. ... You can have no conception of the intense glare here. It is bad in India, but nothing to this. The number of people who are blind or one eyed proves the effect it has upon the sight. You hardly ever see an Arab with sound and perfect eyes.

Before their departure, the new Governor of Bombay, the Honourable Mountstuart Elphinstone, ordered the destruction of all fortifications. This done, Thompson handed over his duties to Sheikh Sultan bin Saqr, whom the British had restored in April 1820 as the principal sheikh, replacing Hassan bin Rahman. Captain Thompson was the first British Political Agent in the region and the only one ever to have been based, albeit briefly, in Ras Al Khaimah. His name and the critical role he played in that historic treaty – which resulted in 150 years of British exclusive control of foreign affairs in return for protection from any external aggression – has, however, faded with the passing of the years. He actually brought with him copies of the Bible translated into Arabic, presumably in the hope of converting some of the local people, but there is no record of any such conversions.

Article 3 of the 'General Treaty for the Cessation of Plunder and Piracy by Land or Sea, dated 5 February, 1820' laid down a condition that a red flag with a white border would be carried by land and sea to identify friendly Arabs. To this day, the same flag flies proudly in Ras Al Khaimah and Sharjah, but other states later modified their flags as it was felt the original mainly represented the Qawasim.

In return for an assurance from the Qawasim to relinquish any ambition to re-establish their maritime force, the British guaranteed the independence and security of the six states in the region: Abu Dhabi, Ajman, Dubai, Ras Al Khaimah, Sharjah and Umm Al Quwain. (Fujairah was recognised as independent of Sharjah by the British government only in 1952.)

A number of highly respected historians argue persuasively that the Qawasim were the victims of Britain's driving ambition to control all trade and sea routes in the area. Whatever the rights and wrongs of either side, the force used by the British to end the Qawasim maritime operation is hard to justify. The Qawasim were undoubtedly an obstacle to the British desire to defend and increase its monopoly in the area through the East India Company. The serious threat the Qawasim posed to achieving this trade domination was, in all probability, the primary reason for the naval invasions.

The signing of the 1820 treaty certainly brought peace and maritime stability to the Gulf, but on land the border and tribal disputes continued. These internal conflicts, which were not covered by any of the treaties signed with the British, were still numerous even when I first arrived in 1959. However, British 'protection' meant that the territorial ambitions of other nations, in particular the Ottoman Turks, were curtailed. Importantly, it also ensured the survival and independence of some of the smaller states, which otherwise could well have been incorporated into their more powerful neighbours.

In 1853, the rather vague terms of previous treaties with the British were clarified by the Perpetual Maritime Truce. The treaty confirmed the banning of maritime hostilities, and also resulted in a new name for the area: the 'Trucial States'.

In December 1887, new 'Exclusive Treaties' were added to the existing ones, in which the rulers agreed for the first time that they would never 'cede, sell, mortgage or give for occupation any part of their territories' without British consent. These new treaties even went so far as to insist that the rulers would have no dealings whatsoever with any other foreign countries without British say-so. This restrictive agreement remained in force right up until independence at the end of 1971, when the British government finally relinquished all prior treaties to allow the States to manage their own affairs.

Since Britain only ever guaranteed their external security, the seven Trucial States were left alone to manage their internal affairs with little support from the British government. One exception, however, was the formation in 1951 of the locally based military force known as the Trucial Oman Levies, which initially consisted of trained soldiers, mostly from Aden, with a few from Jordan. The title Levies had, in the past, been given to local, conscripted, colonial forces in Iraq and Sudan, and the Aden Protectorate Levies were formed on 1 April 1928. The Trucial Oman Levies were renamed the Trucial Oman Scouts in 1956 to emphasise their status as a professional, volunteer fighting unit tasked with ensuring internal safety and security within the seven States. This unique force only came into being after lengthy talks between the Foreign Office and the Ministry of Defence, and took its orders not from the British Middle East Army HQ in Aden, but from the Political Resident based in Bahrain. From these humble beginnings, the Trucial Oman Scouts would bring about the internal peace and stability necessary to achieve the union of the seven States in less than 20 years. It was a remarkable achievement, only made possible thanks to the dedicated officers and men, both Arab and British, who, like me, were fortunate enough to have served in this very special force.

A GENERAL TO THE RESCUE

O n a cold January morning in 1957, my father accompanied me to Fareham railway station to see me off for the start of my call-up in the British Army. I had been persuaded by a smooth-talking recruiting sergeant to sign on for three years, rather than the compulsory two years' National Service, as it meant I could select the regiment in which I wished to serve. It also entitled me to receive a far more generous payment than the 30 shillings per week handed out to National Serviceman. I remembered my elder brother Roger's disappointment when he had been enlisted for his National Service into the Royal Signals and not our county regiment, the Royal Hampshires, so, for the sake of an extra year and more cash in my pocket, I was happy to sign on the dotted line.

I was looking forward to my military basic training at Lower Barracks, Winchester, the training depot for the Royal Hampshires, which had been my first choice. I had been born and educated in Portsmouth, Hampshire, and lived there for all but a couple of my 18 years. At the height of the bombing raids in the Second World War, Portsmouth was targeted on a regular basis as it was an important strategic naval base. The German bombers inflicted terrible casualties and destruction, including on two houses occupied by my mother, brother and me. Fortunately, on both occasions we had been out when the bombs fell, returning later to find our home a pile of rubble. Not wanting to chance our luck for a third time, my brother and I were evacuated to the humble mining home of our mother's parents in the Rhondda Valley, South Wales.

On returning to England towards the end of the war, Roger and I both attended Portsmouth Grammar School. During my schooldays I was far more interested in the school's Cadet Force and sporting activities than boring classroom studies, and was considered to be something of a rebel by the staff. This resulted in my being frequently on the receiving end of the gym shoe or cane, both of which were liberally used by the staff and school prefects alike. Sadly, my long-suffering parents, who had made enormous sacrifices to send both Roger and me to such an outstanding school, had to read my invariably indifferent end-of-term reports, which routinely stated that 'Neild has the potential to do far better than the average results he has achieved'.

Naively, I presumed that my time in the Combined Cadet Force and my physical fitness would make the rigours of the basic training I was about to undertake a stroll in the park. This illusion was about to be rudely shattered, but at the time I eagerly awaited the challenges that lay ahead. My Queen and country were calling.

Those first few days in the cold, damp barracks, being hounded from dawn to dusk by NCOs who took delight in reducing even the most resilient of us to quivering wrecks, were hard to endure. I often heard muffled crying in the few hours of darkness before bracing myself for another day of insults and humiliation. Gradually, most of us came to terms with the discipline. However, the dreadful food dished out to us at mealtimes was something else and I was grateful for my extra few shillings, which I could spend in the NAAFI on Mars bars and packets of crisps.

While basic training was a harsh physical introduction to military life, it did bring me into contact with youths from backgrounds very different from my own. Once we accepted each other as equals, with a common determination not to be broken by our aggressive NCOs, we began to work as a team – although I occasionally had to prove that a 'posh' accent should not be mistaken for a sign of weakness in character or physical strength.

It came as a complete surprise to me that several of our intake were illiterate. Once mutual respect was established, I would be asked to read their incoming mail to them and reply on their behalf, often to their girlfriends depicting in graphic terms what they were missing most. The comic books *Dandy* and *Beano* were the recruits' most popular reading material, with little demand for even tabloid newspapers. It also came as shock to me to see some of these tough young men fainting at the sight of the needle about to be plunged into them as they lined up for our numerous injections. It made me wonder how they would perform in a bayonet charge!

After the first couple of weeks in our ill-fitting uniforms and 'short back and sides' haircuts, we gradually adjusted to our new lives and worked well together. The comradeship established between young men with such varied backgrounds was quite remarkable and I believe can be achieved only in the forces. For the first time, I learned to appreciate the importance of a good education and a close, loving family, something that in the past I had taken for granted. I adjusted reasonably well to all the challenges of basic training and was eventually selected for potential officer training at Wessex Brigade Depot at Topsham Barracks, Exeter. I was genuinely sad to leave behind the recruits I had come to know and respect after all we had gone through together. They all wished me well, but jokingly made it abundantly clear that, should I meet up with them again as an officer, they would refuse to call me 'Sir' or salute me.

At Topsham Barracks I was in a squad of about 30 men from similar backgrounds, all hoping to beat the odds and finally obtain the Queen's commission. The training here was equally hard, and several of my fellow intake failed to make it past the first hurdle. Tragically, one committed suicide in the ablution block and it was left to us to clean up the bloody mess after the body had been removed.

Finally, those of us who made it to the end of our training were sent off, a few at a time each week, to face the War Office Selection Board. There we would be closely scrutinised and put through our paces to ascertain if we were suitable for Officer Cadet training. It was impossible to predict the outcome of the selection board. Of our intake, those we thought to be the most likely to pass actually failed, and others we considered rank outsiders were selected. I was certainly not overconfident that I would pass but, when I was successful, I realised for the first time in my life that hard work and determination to succeed would pay off.

However, my initial euphoria at being selected was very short-lived. I had signed on for three years on the understanding that, on completion of the officer training course, I would receive a short-service three-year commission. It was only after passing the selection board that I was told for the first time that there was a regulation in force that barred those with a short-service commission from serving in the infantry. My friendly and persuasive recruiting sergeant had somehow 'forgotten' to point this out to me. This meant I finished up being sent to the Mons Officer Cadet School instead of Eaton Hall, which was for infantry officer cadets only. The four-month course was tough but rewarding, with the emphasis on our responsibilities to those unfortunate soldiers who would be under our command. It was constantly drummed into us that 'there are no bad soldiers, only bad officers'. On successful completion of my Officer Cadet course in March 1958, I was commissioned into the Royal Army Service Corps (RASC) and, to my delight, posted to Singapore.

The 21-day sea voyage from Southampton on the troopship SS *Nevasa* turned out to be a most enjoyable journey. I shared a cabin with John Lodge, a young Military Police subaltern, also just commissioned, who was on his way to Hong Kong. Once we had passed through the choppy waters of the Bay of Biscay, more passengers emerged after spells of sea sickness, and it became apparent to our observant eyes that the majority of them were unaccompanied wives. John and I have maintained our friendship now for over 50 years and meet up from time to time, mainly in South Africa, for a game of golf. After the game, which is fiercely competitive, our conversation inevitably turns to our sea voyage all those years ago. Suffice to say that for two young, fit bachelors it was a long, demanding but pleasurable voyage.

Despite the attractions of the Far East, being involved in suppressing civil riots in Singapore and being in charge of convoys up to the 'sharp end' in Malaya, I remained as determined as ever to become an infantry officer. I had seen at first hand the vital role carried out by the RASC, and it was a well-accepted fact that fighting troops could not survive and operate without its logistical support. I was thoroughly enjoying the military life and my important responsibilities, but this never shook my desperate desire to be deployed in a more active role, which could only be satisfied by serving in the infantry.

There were, however, three little obstacles standing in my way. The first was to obtain a regular commission, the second was to secure the signature of my commanding officer (CO) approving my transfer from the RASC to the infantry, and the third was to find an infantry regiment willing to accept me.

Fortunately, the first hurdle was soon cleared. After only six months in Singapore, I submitted my request to my CO to be considered for a regular commission. Much to my surprise and delight, this was immediately approved and I was on my way back to the UK. On arrival, I was posted to a Transport Company in the beautiful city of Chester, where I was to prepare myself for the Regular Commission Board. The one pip on my shoulder now had a GSM Malaya medal on my chest for company, which I wore proudly, although I was not sure if it was really justified after only a few months of operational duties. However, my next task was to pass the War Office Selection Board for a second time and to convince them that I was worthy of a future in the Regular Army.

Miraculously, I passed the three-day selection board – despite the embarrassment of sporting a black eye and swollen lip, obtained the night before the start. Two of us had decided to go out for a drink instead of concentrating, like all the others, on the three crucial days that we were about to face. We entered a rural pub and it quickly became apparent that the presence of two 'posh young gentlemen' was not welcome to all the locals. A rowdy, belligerent group of about six took it upon themselves to assist us In leaving and a fight began. The two of us more than held our own but, the next morning, before the selection board tests began, we were marched in front of the board commanding officer. He could scarcely believe his eyes at the state of us and told us in no uncertain words that such behaviour and our bruised and battered faces had not got us off to the best of starts. For good measure, he stated that our chances of passing were practically zero. Despite this initial setback, neither of us threw in the towel and, incredibly, we both passed and obtained our Regular Commissions. This gave me a two-year head start over other young officers of similar age, but it has always been a personal regret that I missed out on Sandhurst and its proud traditions.

I have never been a great believer in fate but, ever since the following incident, I am more inclined to keep an open mind about it. At Chester, I had confided in our Chief Clerk that it was my ambition to become an infantry officer and he promised to help me should the right posting materialise. Soon after this conversation, he informed me there was a vacancy for a Transport Officer to be seconded to the Trucial Oman Scouts (TOS), headquartered in Sharjah in the Trucial States. I had neither heard of this force nor had any idea where Sharjah or the Trucial States were. The only relevant detail for me was that the TOS was commanded by an infantry officer. His name was Colonel Stewart Carter, and he had a Military Cross to his name for good measure. The Chief Clerk did point out to me that the vacancy was for an experienced officer and, with only a modest one year of commissioned service, it was highly unlikely that I would be considered. While the two of us were scheming how to resolve this little obstacle, it was announced that our unit was to receive an official visit by no less a personage than the Commander of the RASC himself.

Leading up to this all-important day, everything that moved was painted, polished or saluted, and fortunately the big day went off smoothly. When I was introduced to the general, he congratulated me on obtaining my Regular Commission and asked me what future ambitions I hoped to achieve. Making the most of this golden opportunity, I promptly replied that I was keen to be considered for the Transport Officer vacancy with the TOS that had recently become available. He thought about this for a moment, before replying that I was probably too young and inexperienced but that there was no harm in applying.

No sooner had the exhaust pipe of his staff car disappeared through the main gates than my application, freshly signed by my CO, was left in the safe and capable hands of the Chief Clerk. He forwarded it through the red tape and formalities to the decision-makers, adding, with tongue in cheek, that the general himself was aware of my application and had given his personal approval that this application should be given careful consideration. I will be eternally grateful to that Chief Clerk for his assistance and the slight exaggeration of my conversation with the general.

A short time later, to my great joy and surprise, I received official confirmation that I was to be seconded to the TOS as the Transport Officer. Call it fate, luck or being in the right place at the right time, but, early in 1959, at the tender age of 20, I was about to become the youngest British officer ever to serve with the Trucial Oman Scouts.

At the time, my selfish thoughts were concentrated purely on the fact that in the TOS I would have an infantry CO. This meant that, provided I made a good impression and my new CO agreed to sign my transfer application from the RASC, I would have overcome the second obstacle to becoming an infantry officer. Little did I know that I was about to embark on an Arabian journey which would change my life forever.

SHARJAH AND BEYOND

In the brief period before bidding my parents farewell and heading off for the unknown desert sands, I did try and research the region and the force in which I was about to serve. There was little to be found, and in April 1959 I flew to Bahrain on an RAF VC-10 with no idea of what to expect or the conditions to be faced. When I stepped off the plane, after many hours, the incredible heat hit me head-on and literally took my breath away. It was a powerful introduction to the scorching temperatures I would have to learn to endure. Bahrain, the stop-off for Sharjah in those days, only had one hotel, the Speedbird, which was owned by BOAC. It was popular not only because there was no alternative, but also because it was where the aircrews and (more importantly) the air hostesses stayed when they had to stop over. The other few facilities in that area, which I only discovered on later visits, included the Royal Navy base (HMS Jufair) and an American oil camp, both of which allowed us to visit and watch films at their open-air cinemas, a welcome luxury in those days.

After spending a night at the Speedbird Hotel, I flew on an RAF Pembroke aircraft to Sharjah, which had the only airport in the Trucial States. It was also home to a large RAF contingent, a squadron of cavalry which, at that time, was the Life Guards, as well as the barracks and the HQ of my new force, the Trucial Oman Scouts. My initial observation was that this was far more basic even than Bahrain, and that the base was surrounded in all directions by sand, followed by more sand and dwellings made out of palm-tree branches, known as *barastis*. It was like nothing I had ever seen, and I began to question the wisdom of volunteering to serve in such a remote part of the world. My first impression was that, apart from the military presence, nothing had changed here for centuries.

Upon my arrival, I was taken to meet the adjutant, Captain John Savage, and was amazed to find that he was an old friend of my brother's and had been a school prefect at our old school (Portsmouth Grammar) when I was still a young pupil. He briefed me on what was to be expected of me and the important role the TOS played in the Gulf. He left me in no doubt that a high standard of military discipline was expected at all times and that we British officers were to respect the beliefs and customs of our Arab soldiers.

This meeting was followed by my introduction to the Transport Squadron commander, Major Don Merrylees, a well-built and athletic-looking officer. Understandably, he did not appear to be overly impressed with his very young and inexperienced new second-in-command. We went by Land Rover, the main means of transport, to the Officers' Mess, located in a splendid old colonial-style building on the edge of the Sharjah creek. Here I was introduced to Sergeant Iqbal, and left in his more-than-capable hands. I soon discovered that he ran everything to do with the Officers' Mess and did so in a most orderly and efficient manner. He allocated me a room on the ground floor, fortunately as far away as possible from the long-drop latrines which, despite the efforts of the 'latrine wallahs', were particularly smelly, especially in the hot months. A tailor took my measurements and, within 24 hours, I was kitted out, rather self-consciously, in my new uniform, complete with the red-and-white *shemagh* Arab headdress. I looked like a very poor impersonation of Lawrence of Arabia.

I was appointed temporary captain on arrival and, because I was by far the youngest seconded British officer ever to serve in the Scouts, everyone felt rather sorry for me and went out of their way to help and guide me as much as they could. No doubt Sergeant Iqbal bore this in mind when he decided on an orderly for me, which was when the long-suffering Gus entered my life. In *Arabian Days,* the informative book by Mike Curtis and Tony Cawston on their time in the TOS, Mike described Gus as resembling Quasimodo with a pistol, which was a fair description. I never did find out if Gus had the pistol to protect me or to keep me in my place but, whichever it was, it worked and Gus was my protective shadow for the entire time I spent in the Gulf. A more true, devoted and loyal friend would have been impossible to find.

Don Merrylees was incredibly patient with me and certainly never showed his probable dismay at having such an inexperienced youngster who was supposed to assist him, but was more likely to be a liability. Don had an easy-going manner and was popular with all those under his command. I would learn a great deal from him, especially in dealing with our Arab soldiers. He had the natural ability to laugh and joke with everyone and at the same time leave no one in any doubt as to the severe consequences of failing to comply with the high standards on which he insisted. Fortunately, we also had some excellent British NCOs transferred to us, who discreetly attempted to teach me about the vehicle problems caused by the heat and sand and the warning signs to look out for. This advice helped me enormously when I carried out routine vehicle inspections in order to try and give the impression that I knew what I was doing. To this day, I am completely hopeless when it comes to anything mechanical, and I doubt if I fooled anyone in those days either.

There were also plenty of highly efficient and helpful Arab NCOs, who kindly and painstakingly gave me vital lessons in their customs and tribal backgrounds. This was also essential for me to begin to understand the men with whom I had the privilege of serving. The senior Arab NCO was Sergeant Yusuf Eid who ruled the squadron with a rod of iron.

Before joining the Scouts, most officers were sent on an Arabic language course, which was understandably a prerequisite if you were to communicate with your men, as hardly any of them spoke English. Unfortunately, I had been thrown in at the deep end and, on top of my lack of mechanical knowledge, could not speak or understand a single word of Arabic. I was determined to learn the basic language as soon as possible, which I did manage to do, but only after a great deal of assistance from my soldiers, who would collapse in laughter at my attempts to master Arabic words with my pronounced English accent.

The Trucial Oman Scouts had originally been formed in 1951 as the Trucial Oman Levies, as a force of some 100 men under the command of a Major Hankin-Turvin. The major had been seconded from the Arab Legion on the recommendation of its famous commander, General Glub Pasha. In March 1956, the force was renamed the Trucial Oman Scouts and their initial role was to maintain peace and goodwill in the Trucial States as well as to suppress slave trafficking and provide a military protective escort for any British political representative. The UK Treasury had agreed to provide a budget of £35,000 to form a 'small body of armed police'. From these humble beginnings, the TOS expanded significantly and eventually played a vital role in ensuring a smooth and peaceful transition during the formation of the United Arab Emirates less than 20 years later.

After a couple of days spent settling in, it was time to meet the TOS Commander, Colonel Stewart Carter MC. At the time I arrived in Sharjah, a great deal of anti-British propaganda was being broadcast from a radio station called *Sawt al Arab* ('Voice of the Arabs'), in which Colonel Carter was frequently reported as having been killed in action – obviously intended to reduce the morale of our soldiers. The only way to counter these false reports was for the Colonel to make a whistle-stop tour of all the rifle squadrons, spread out over the entire region, so that everyone could see him and then cheer at the good news of his survival. On one occasion, an old soldier standing next to me was shaking his head in disbelief when he saw the triumphant and very much alive Colonel Carter acknowledging the cheers from his men. When I asked him what the problem was, he replied that he had worked out that a stock of Colonel Carters was kept in a military quartermaster's store in Aden and, as one died, he was replaced with another! On another occasion, after the Colonel had once again been reported to have passed on, he ordered the flags to be flown at half-mast as a sign of respect. Not only was he a great commander, but he also possessed a fine sense of humour.

He was a striking man, with a face that somehow reminded me of the features of a hawk, and I realised immediately that I was in the presence of a very special man. It was clear that his unique style of command and leadership had deservedly won him the respect and loyalty of all those who were fortunate to serve under him. He quickly put me at my ease, and eventually asked why I had volunteered to serve in the Scouts at such a young age. Believing honesty to be by far the best option, I explained my ambition to join an infantry regiment, which could only be achieved with the recommendation of my CO. This would have been virtually impossible to obtain while I was serving with my original Corps. It had therefore been necessary to find another unit to achieve this aim, and I hoped the TOS and my new CO would oblige.

He thought this was highly amusing, and said that he would keep the details of my intended objective between the two of us, and 'keep an eye' on me and make a decision about my request to be considered for the infantry in due course.

To gain the discreet support of my CO, provided I met with his approval in the months to come, was a huge step forward. It was now imperative that my Corps did not discover my true reason for joining the TOS, as they could well have blocked any later application for transfer, in which case my hopes of becoming an infantry officer would be gone forever.

A few days after this, the Colonel called me up to say that the two of us would spend the afternoon fishing together. I noted that it was not a question of whether I liked or enjoyed fishing, and I was clearly expected to go with him. The truth was that I had never been fishing in my life, but I could only presume that the Colonel took it for granted that officers went fishing. We went off to a nearby seashore, where I was handed a rod and a tin of bait was placed between us. Carefully watching what the Colonel did, I followed his actions and eventually managed to get a worm on my hook and, somehow, cast into the sea. I felt a nibble on my line and excitedly reeled it in, only to find a naked hook with no fish. This happened several times, and I could see the Colonel beginning to glance at me frequently with a bewildered look as he was catching fish the whole time. Eventually, too embarrassed to keep taking new bait, I just stood there with the rod in the water, resigned to the fact that I had absolutely no chance of catching anything. I was very relieved when the Colonel called it a day. Fortunately, he never asked me to go fishing again and, no doubt, had seen through my pathetic pretence to be the complete fisherman. I had sleepless nights contemplating whether being a competent angler was a prerequisite for the Colonel's support for my infantry dreams.

To get from the military camp to the Officers' Mess on the creek, one had to drive on sandy tracks for about 20 minutes through the spread-out small town of Sharjah. On this journey we also had to pass the Ruler's fort, complete with a couple of cannon, which was recognised as the town centre. It was here, on a Friday after prayers, that the townsfolk would gather if there were any offenders sentenced for punishment. The unfortunate prisoner would be stripped to the waist and tied to the cannon, which would be extremely hot, having been exposed to the midday sun. One of the Ruler's tall, black bodyguards would normally carry out the beating using a cane, with the crowd shouting out the number of lashes. I was quite impressed, when, the first time I witnessed this brutal but effective form of punishment, the beating was stopped before the full number of strokes because the man had fainted. I soon discovered, however, that this was not for compassionate reasons, when a bucket of water was thrown over the offender to bring him round so that he felt every strike of the cane when the beating resumed. On completion of the sentence, the man would literally be peeled from the cannon, leaving behind layers of skin on the metal. Understandably, crime was virtually unheard of in the territory, and the majority of offenders were illegal immigrants who had come to the Gulf seeking work.

I once witnessed the public execution of a man who had been convicted of murder. He had come back after a long absence, working away from home, to discover that his wife and children had moved in with another man. That same night, he poured petrol around the *barasti* house and set light to it, killing all the inhabitants. I was told that the only reason he was sentenced to death was that he had killed the children as well. If he had only killed the adulterous couple, he would probably have received a much more lenient sentence – and possibly not have been prosecuted for any crime at all! There was a huge crowd to witness this execution, including a few of us more bloodthirsty, curious types. Our Medical Officer joined us, though I was not quite sure what assistance he thought he would be able to give to the condemned prisoner. When the man was brought out, there was silence as the crime and sentence were read out. He seemed resigned to his fate and just stood there quietly until one of the Ruler's guards approached and shot him with a rifle at very short range. A Land Rover then appeared, the corpse was tied to it and then off went the vehicle, dragging the man behind in the direction of the desert, where I presume he was either buried or left for the vultures.

We had a shooting incident in the Sharjah camp one day. The Motor Transport Squadron, where I was based, was located opposite the resident rifle squadron. Early one morning, I suddenly heard the distinct sound of a rifle shot, followed by a great deal of excited shouting. I hurried out of my office to see what was happening, and saw the soldier who had obviously fired the shot, calmly standing there. He made no effort to resist me when I took the weapon off him and ordered his arrest. It transpired that he had simply entered a barrack room, shot the soldier he was looking for, and then waited patiently to be taken into custody. It was eventually established that there was a blood feud between the two families and, in his opinion, he (the accused soldier) had acted in an honourable way. Normally, when something like this happened, the family of the deceased could claim blood money or the right to shoot the culprit, but this was not an option as both were serving soldiers, subject to military law. A Board of Inquiry was held and the court came to the conclusion that the accused was unfit to stand trial due to insanity; he was sent to a mental hospital in Aden. The family of the deceased would not have agreed with, or even understood, this verdict, and it may well have led to more bloodshed, as family feuds resulting in fatalities were very common at that time.

Being based in Sharjah was relatively pleasant, since we had a great Officers' Mess with a balcony looking across the creek, catching any welcome breeze. However, the smell of drying coral, used in the building of the more substantial residences, was a touch strong for the more sensitive noses. Our individual rooms came complete with fans and air conditioning, which I would soon discover was far better than the 'comforts' of the outstations. Sometimes, officers from these outstations would come back to Sharjah just to spend a couple of days in the air conditioning, to ease the irritation of their prickly heat or sunburn.

Back at our camp, the Staff and HQ officers also had air-conditioned offices, but we lesser mortals had to make do with our basic *barasti* offices. The only relief from the heat was the occasional hint of a cooling wind finding its way through the date-palm walls. Unfortunately, this welcome breeze was usually accompanied by innumerable flies. The only way for us to survive and get through the paperwork was to start work as soon as it was light and, after a couple of hours, return to the Mess for breakfast and a paludrine tablet for malaria. By about 11 am, any attempt at writing was a waste of time because the constant flow of perspiration turned the paper into a soggy mess. Back once more to the Mess to consume gallons of delicious fresh lime and lemon, followed by lunch and a siesta. At about 4 pm, we would go back to the camp to try and catch up on any administrative duties that still needed to be carried out. Frequently, we would still be working in our offices in the relative cool of the evening with the help of a hurricane lamp.

I like to think that, with a great deal of assistance from my Arab NCOs, I became reasonably proficient in my Arabic, but engines and how they worked remained a mystery to me. Don wisely made sure my duties concentrated, as much as possible, on administration, as serious repercussions could flow from vehicles breaking down in the desert.

We were fortunate to be living at our comfortable Officers' Mess, complete with a generator and long-drop latrine facilities. Our very near neighbours in Sharjah town were not so lucky. They had to make do with their *barasti* homes and the coastline for sanitation and ablution. Small children would look at us with great curiosity when we travelled outside the base, but any attempt to smile or greet them would have them scurrying back behind their veiled mothers, dressed from head to toe in black. The children, and possibly their mothers, found this all very amusing, but only at a safe distance from these strange white men.

Our life was exciting and certainly never routine, and the majority of Scouts officers were great characters and good soldiers. However, with a few exceptions, they were not motivated by career prospects or promotion. I recall that, on one occasion, a Royal Navy ship based in Bahrain was patrolling in the Gulf and had invited us British TOS officers on board for a very social party. Eventually we made our farewells and returned to shore, well aware of the generous amount we had been 'forced' to consume. Next morning, I realised that Don Merrylees was missing; there was no sign of him in his room at the Mess, so a search was made. Later that morning, it was discovered that Don had enjoyed naval hospitality to the full and had found a quiet spot on board the ship to 'sleep it off'. Unfortunately, none of us knew about this and the ship had sailed back to Bahrain, which is where Don woke up. He flew back the following day and, when I met him off the plane, his opening remark was 'Have I been missed?' I am sure that, anywhere else, this incident would have had Don facing up to the full might of military discipline, but the Scouts were in many ways a law unto themselves. Don was subjected only to a verbal reprimand and probably some extra duties by Colonel Carter who, more than likely, had difficulty suppressing a smile when delivering his reprimand. We were convinced that the 'blue jobs' had deliberately taken Don hostage, and so we planned our revenge, which would have involved the desert and camels. Wisely, they declined an invitation to join us at our Officers' Mess at a later date, giving some feeble excuse.

During this time in Sharjah, I became very friendly with Desmond Cosgrove from the King's Regiment, a staff officer on the intelligence team. His mother was from the Middle East and he had inherited his Arab looks from her. He was not only totally fluent in Arabic but also had an immaculate English accent. He told me about when he went to Bahrain, dressed in his TOS uniform, to greet a contingent from his regiment that was due to arrive there by sea. Apparently, two young King's Regiment subalterns were overheard saying that they had met an Arab officer on board who not only spoke immaculate English but also knew all about the regiment. When I got to know Desmond better, I confided to him that my greatest wish was to be accepted by an infantry regiment, should Colonel Carter sign the necessary application. Typically for Desmond, he promised to help if possible.

People frequently look at me in amazement when I describe what the Gulf was like only 50 years ago, and mention that there was hardly any real social life. The Scouts Ball was held once a year, and single young ladies from as far away as Bahrain and Aden were flown in by the RAF to attend this popular function. A grand time was had by all. Twenty-four hours later, with tearful farewells and promises to keep in touch, the female guests departed and we returned to our monastic Bedouin life once more.

Even in the late 1950s, the Trucial States region was still virtually unknown as a destination for foreigners, but there was a handful of expatriates in Dubai. I remember great characters like Lt Col Dr Desmond McCaully, the Senior Medical Officer for the Trucial States, Bill Duff, the financial advisor to the Ruler of Dubai, Eric Tulloch, the water engineer, and George Chapman from Gray Mackenzie. We regularly socialised with them but, on occasions, had great difficulty in finding our way back to Sharjah late at night after their generous hospitality. There were no road signs and, with numerous sand tracks to choose from, it was not unknown for late-night revellers to end up on the way to Al Ain, 125-kilometres inland, or some other equally remote place.

Travelling around was not straightforward, even in daytime. There was not one single tarmac road in the country and it was comparatively easy to get lost or stuck in *sabka* (salt flats), even when making the journey from Sharjah to Dubai. There were no bridges in Dubai, so one had to cross the creek in small boats known as *abras*. Apart from the *souq* (market), there was only one shop, Jashanmals, which specialised in imported goods. Here one could purchase books, records and other luxury goods. I am delighted to see that, from such a modest start, Jashanmals has flourished and can now be found in shopping malls across the region. My daughter, Michelle, still has some old, sand-scratched long-playing records I bought from that lone store all those years ago, which she still plays from time to time. Another popular local store in Dubai was 'Captain's Store'. This was located on the edge of the creek and owned by a local man, very small in stature, who was a great character and a close associate of Sheikh Rashid, the Ruler of Dubai. 'Captain' was frequently included in the entourage of His Highness when he was travelling overseas, and he was also a very talented photographer. Somewhere there doubtless lies a treasure trove of photographs that he took during his time in the company of Sheikh Rashid.

Although there was a busy gold *souq* in Dubai, we purchased our gold cufflinks and ladies' jewellery in Sharjah, from an Iraqi who also made the silver cap badges and *khanjars* (daggers) for our uniforms. His name was Adam Naim but, with typical military humour, we always referred to him as 'Robin B', implying that he charged us outrageous prices. In reality this was very unfair, as he looked after us extremely well.

Dubai's main income in those days came from gold 'smuggling', which was quite legal. Gold would be flown out from London and then transferred by *dhows* (wooden sailing vessels) to a meeting point in international waters for boats from India. These transactions were highly popular and profitable because it was illegal for Indians to possess gold, so they were keen to buy it from the Dubai *dhows*. The Indians paid for the gold bullion in silver, which the *dhows* would take back to Dubai. The silver would then be flown back to London and exchanged for gold at a huge profit, and the process would start all over again. Because of this lucrative bullion trade, Dubai quickly became known as the City of Gold and, in the late 1960s, only France and Switzerland imported more gold from London. One of the main reasons given for the construction of Dubai International Airport at the end of 1960 was that the Dubai merchants were not happy about paying import duties to Sharjah, which was the only airport available to them. It was also far more convenient for the gold to be flown directly to Dubai for easy onward travel to the waiting dhows in the Dubai creek. This airport, which was constructed by Costain, had a 1,800-metre long runway of compacted sand which was capable of supporting a Douglas DC-3 aircraft. It also boasted a small airport terminal, handling the few passengers who arrived there. I often think back to those humble beginnings when I arrive at today's magnificent Dubai International Airport, with its fantastic facilities, standing 'patiently' in the queue along with hundreds of other disembarking passengers waiting to clear Immigration and Customs!

It was common knowledge who the big gold smugglers were, and many made a considerable fortune, long before the discovery of oil. In those days, it was possible to buy into a shipment with an opportunity to make good money in a few days. However, I was never personally tempted as I learned that, occasionally, a dhow carrying the precious metal would be caught and the cargo confiscated, probably to keep the Indian authorities happy. You could virtually guarantee that this would happen only to a *dhow* financed by get-rich-quick investors and not the professional, high-powered men with the right connections.

To my total surprise, after only a few months in Sharjah with the Transport Squadron, I was informed by Colonel Carter that I was to be posted to B Rifle Squadron as second-in-command. I could not believe my good fortune as not only was B Squadron located in Al Ain (which was probably the most popular location to serve in the region), but it was commanded by another Scout legend, Major Ian Maxwell Craig-Adams. There were four rifle squadrons in the TOS, each commanded by a seconded British Army major who was supported by one or two captains. At that time, in the late 1950s, there were no Arabs with UK officer training, and the few *Mulazims* (a local Arab officer rank) who were part of the squadrons had their own Officers' Mess. 'Shiny B', as B Squadron was affectionately known, did not have another British captain when I arrived. Ian had been on his own for a short time, commanding more than 100 soldiers, and administration had been a very low priority.

As already mentioned, travel was precarious on any track, but to take on the sand dunes and arrive successfully in Buraimi, as the area was known, some eight hours later was no mean feat. It was always better to leave as early in the morning as possible, when the sand was still cold and the tyres could get a firmer grip. Once the temperature rose, the sand became very hot and one had to deflate the tyres to attempt to negotiate steep inclines. It was also tiring to have to inflate the tyres again, using only a very basic foot pump that was not renowned for its efficiency, especially in soft sand.

It was essential, before setting off from one location to another, to sign out at the signal centre. The personnel there would send your time of departure by Morse code message to your destination, where staff would be ready to send out a search party should you fail to arrive on time. The signal centre at our HQ in Sharjah was manned by boy soldiers as Morse operators. Their speed and efficiency never ceased to amaze us and visitors alike, especially as few of them spoke any English and had little or no idea what the message was all about.

Having booked out at daybreak, my faithful orderly Gus and I set off in a B Squadron Land Rover that had been sent in the day before to collect us. I am still fascinated by the beauty of the desert, and the sense of space and emptiness that is rather similar to looking out over a vast expanse of sea. Of course, in those days, en route one would pass wells, with Bedouin women and children fetching water for their families and the presence of camels and goats, a scene that had not changed for generations. There would also be the occasional camel convoy transporting goods from one area to another. Sadly, these are now distant memories, apart from in very remote areas, but I remember them with great nostalgia. I also have to accept that the women are probably much happier today turning on a tap, and goods are transported to market more efficiently by lorries along the extensive dual carriageways; that is progress.

Gus and I eventually arrived, weary but excited, at the formidable and impressive entrance to Fort Jahili with its cannon and armed guards. Its gleaming white walls made the fort look like something out of *Beau Geste* and, in the far corner, standing majestically on its own, was a two-tiered tower that was the Officers' Mess. Looking down at me from the parapet, with cigarette in one hand and a glass of whisky in the other, was Major Ian Maxwell Craig-Adams.

It is hard to do justice to Ian in any description except that he was big in every sense of the word. He was absolutely adored by his soldiers, and he felt the same towards to them. Ian had served in the Indian Army and was a real colonial in behaviour and outlook; he was also a highly professional soldier who had little time for administration and paperwork. That evening, the two of us sat down together and Ian firmly but pleasantly told me what was and was not expected of me, all of which made good common sense. Ian had a well-deserved reputation for enjoying a drink and a cigarette and I noticed the whisky level going down at a rapid rate as he chain-smoked from a round tin containing 50 Player's Perfectos Finos. He eventually fell asleep in his chair, snoring loudly, and I was not sure what to do. Should I leave him there and face a reprimand in the morning for not waking him? I made the mistake of gently disturbing him and, the next thing I knew, was flying through the air like a human cannonball at the circus, landing in a heap on the concrete floor. Ian hurried across to check that I was still in one piece and then warned me against attempting to wake him when sleeping. I assured him that I had learned my lesson, and I never tried to disturb him again.

I also discovered that there was an enormous backlog of administration to be dealt with, because Ian had placed all official correspondence in an overflowing 'pending' file, which was gathering dust in a corner. As already mentioned, he could not be bothered with such trivialities as paperwork and, provided his men were looked after and the squadron was fully operational, he was content and ignored all pleas from HQ in Sharjah to complete their numerous forms in triplicate. Somehow he managed to get away with this, but it had been clearly pointed out to me before my departure from Sharjah to join B Squadron that I was expected to 'clear up the backlog'.

Like all the outstations, we had no electricity and only an old kerosene fridge that would occasionally work if turned upside-down and given a good kick. Because of the temperamental behaviour of the so-called fridge, we had to rely on whatever local fresh rations were available or tinned products. Goat was the only accessible fresh meat and, on rare occasions, we would have fish from the Batinah coast, which would arrive by 'express camel'. It was not possible to keep or store anything for very long, so food had to be eaten there and then, and Ian insisted that almost everything was curried. He loved hot, spicy food and delighted in eating raw chillies. However, the non-stop attack of a red-hot diet was playing havoc with my internal system and I spent many a miserable hour on the isolated loo outside the fort wall. One day, I pleaded with Ian for a change from the daily curry and he agreed, reluctantly, to my suggestion of a cottage pie. My stomach and I were really looking forward to this gastronomic delight and it literally looked good enough to eat – and it was, until I took my first mouthful and discovered that Ian had ordered it to be curried!

The temperature was incredibly high in the summer and with my fair, sensitive skin I found myself frequently suffering from sunburn and prickly heat, which was a very common complaint. I would have thought that, after all the exposure to the sun, my skin would have toughened up, but this was not the case and Johnson's prickly-heat powder and soap continued to be essential items for me. Since my return to live in the Gulf, one of the questions I am asked most frequently is how we managed to cope with the summer heat in those days, and my truthful reply is always 'with great difficulty'.

Fort Jahili has recently been meticulously restored and the internal layout modified to become the Al Ain National Museum. This excellently covers some of Abu Dhabi's early history and its rulers, plus a large section devoted to the incredible travels of Wilfred Thesiger. Today, the fort is surrounded by magnificent hotels, villas and dual carriageways but in those days it stood alone, with only the desert stretching in all directions for company.

Every afternoon, after finishing his curry and a few gins, Ian would head out in his Land Rover for the vast expanse of open desert. His Land Rover had a hand throttle and, having first locked the steering wheel to make a gentle turn, he would set the throttle to a low speed. The Land Rover would then proceed slowly, rotating in a large circle with Ian sitting at the wheel fast asleep, catching any passing breeze and enjoying his siesta. It was a truly unforgettable sight.

Another memorable landmark at the fort for me was my 21st birthday. Ian was out on patrol, so I was on my own with no one to share the celebration. Colonel Carter suddenly appeared with a bottle of Johnnie Walker Black Label, which was virtually impossible to come by at that time. He wished me a happy birthday and then was off once more on his busy travels, but I much appreciated that he had found the time to pop in and see me. I also received a registered letter from my Aunt Blodwyn, my godmother, whose birthday also fell on 1 December. She had married a wealthy, kind banker known to us as Uncle King, who had spent most of his life in South America, but they had never had children of their own. Inside the envelope was a postal order for five pounds, but to my eternal shame I sent it straight back saying that her financial need was obviously greater than mine. Quite rightly, she never forgave me and so I eventually missed out on inheriting a lovely home on the Isle of Wight. Such is the stupidity of youth.

Feeling a bit sorry for myself, and with no one to share the birthday bottle Colonel Carter had brought me, I started drinking the scotch on my own. It was not long before the golden liquid hit the right spots and I started singing a variant of the traditional song: 'I've got the key to the fort, never been twenty-one before!'. Before daybreak the next morning, the faithful Gus woke me and, as I reluctantly raised my tender head, I realised that my pillow was the steering wheel of my Land Rover. I felt considerably older than the day before, and had more than a slight problem focusing on the challenges of the adult world I would have to face in the years to come. Whenever I return to Fort Jahili, the old memories are still vivid in my mind. I always take a quiet moment or two to reflect on the past and remember my time there and all the great characters associated with the fort. The old tower that was our Officers' Mess is now depicted on the 50 dirham UAE banknote and will continue to be a very special place for me and a permanent link with the past.

Fort Jahili in Al Ain is located in the region known as the Buraimi Oasis, an area associated with several major events involving the Trucial Oman Levies. Saudi Arabia had periodically claimed the area, which consisted of nine villages, six belonging to Abu Dhabi and the remaining three to Oman. Saudi Arabia argued that it had occupied the oasis in the 19th century, and in 1949 it again claimed sovereignty of the area, this time supported by the American oil company Aramco. It is probably fair to assume that this claim had more to do with the potential future discovery of oil than historical legitimacy but, in 1952, a small contingent of Saudi soldiers entered and occupied the Omani village of Hamasa. This was followed by a series of attempts to gain the loyalty of the oasis tribesmen by bribery and other means. It is well documented that Sheikh Zayed Al Nahyan, who was the Ruler's Representative in Al Ain at the time, refused an offer of US $42 million to support the Saudi claim. Even today, this is an enormous amount of money, but in those days it would have been hard to resist. However, anyone privileged to have known Sheikh Zayed would have realised that no amount of money would ever have persuaded him, even at that time before oil had been discovered in Abu Dhabi. Sheikh Zayed was blessed with a high moral character, and his love for his people and their homeland could never be doubted – and certainly never bought.

Since the arrival of the Saudis in the Buraimi Oasis, there had been a steady deterioration in the situation on the ground. Several camel caravans had also been intercepted while carrying rice and provisions to the Saudis in the village of Hamasa. Despite constant dialogue and communications on the political front, nothing was being achieved. On 6 November 1953, the Senior British Army Officer in the Gulf felt it necessary to issue an Operational Directive to Lt Colonel Martin, the new Commander of the Trucial Oman Levies, to 'prevent arms, ammunition, supplies and reinforcements from entering the Trucial States and to blockade the Saudis in Hamasa'.

The very next day, a group consisting of Major Thwaites, Flying Officer Duncan (Medical Officer), Regimental Sergeant Major Daud Sidqui, Sergeant Chinn and Corporal Cruikshank arrived at Post 5 in an area between the villages of Buraimi and Saara. Their mission was to investigate a report that some soldiers of the Trucial Oman Levies based there had been selling ammunition. On arrival they were met with armed resistance and Major Thwaites, Flying Officer Duncan and RSM Daud Sidqui were shot dead. Sergeant Chinn, himself wounded, was able to drive to the Squadron HQ with Corporal Cruikshank, who was also seriously hurt, and send an urgent message to the Regimental HQ in Sharjah. Bill Cruikshank, now in his 80s, recalls:

> Charlie (Chinn) and I had gone as usual to do the regular trucks inspection and maintenance at Buraimi on 5 Nov, 1953. The next day we heard a lot of shouting and rifles being waived [sic] about by the Levies. Someone told us they were on

the point of mutiny. That night Major Thwaites told us his squadron was being recalled to Sharjah. He said many of the Levies were dishonest and selling rifle bullets to the local Arabs. Next morning we got up as usual and Major Thwaites told Charlie and I [sic] to be prepared for trouble. He then came back and told us we were to go with him along with the RAF doctor and the Arab Sergeant Major Daud. We were to apprehend three Levies who had refused orders from their officer to return to base. We were to go unarmed to show we had no intention of using force to arrest them. (There were five of us and only three of them!!) As we drove to the desert post 5 we saw three Levies walking along the track away from the post. Major Thwaites stopped some way behind them and walked up to them along with the Doctor and Daud, he signalled to us to join them. I heard Daud shout to the three who stopped as we approached them and they opened up with their rifles. I saw the Major and the Doctor fall, Daud turned to run towards us and he fell. Charlie and I turned and started running to our Morris truck. Charlie fell to the ground as bullets started hitting him, I carried on running, the fastest I had ever run in my life, I jumped into the back of the Morris. Bullets were coming through the canvas top and the truck side, and then going through the petrol tank. I passed out with the fumes. I came to with the truck moving at speed. I had no idea who was driving. When it stopped at the fort I jumped out to see it had been driven by Charlie.

The three Adeni soldiers responsible for this appalling massacre deserted to the Saudis in Hamasa but were eventually returned, thanks to negotiations between Sheikh Zayed and Sheikh Saqr of Buraimi. Because they had carried out this cowardly act on Omani territory, the three soldiers were sent for trial by Sharia law in Muscat. Bill Cruikshank describes the trial as follows:

The trial was somewhat of a mystery to me as it was conducted in Arabic. When I was questioned it was translated back and forth. The three were found guilty and sent to the prison. They could not be executed as the only witness was a Christian – me.

According to reports I have read, the three were found guilty of murder but, for the reason explained by Bill Cruikshank, received indefinite prison sentences in the notorious Jalali prison in Muscat. As a result of this incident, all Adeni soldiers serving in the Trucial Oman Levies were screened, and the vast majority of them were dismissed and sent back to Aden. A new, more sensible policy to recruit local tribesmen from the Trucial States was implemented.

There had been a steady deterioration in the Buraimi Oasis on all sides, which led to a tribunal being set up in Geneva from 1 to 17 September 1955, in an attempt to resolve the situation. Many local chiefs were called and Peter Clayton, a serving officer of the Levies, also gave evidence. The tribunal itself was controversial and most members, including the Belgian chairman, resigned after admitting to having been approached by various parties attempting to influence their decisions. Peter was later to become one of the most respected and knowledgeable authorities on the region, as was made evident in his book *Two Alpha Lima* (the radio call sign of the TOS), which records the history of the first ten years of the force.

On 26 October 1955, the British Prime Minister, Sir Anthony Eden, made a statement in the House of Commons referring to the breakdown of the tribunal in Geneva. He advised that all peaceful negotiations to stop the Saudis from attempting to influence the sovereignty issue of the Buraimi Oasis had failed. He went on to say that forces loyal to the ruler of Abu Dhabi and the Sultan of Muscat, supported by the Trucial Oman Levies, had taken steps to resume their previous control of the Buraimi Oasis and the area to the west of it. He concluded by saying that the military action was regretted but it was hoped that the Saudi government would accept the decision in time, and the British government was ready at all times to discuss 'minor rectifications of the line' in light of local circumstances.

The military action referred to by Sir Antony Eden was the capture of Hamasa village after a prolonged engagement, which resulted in the eviction of the Saudi military presence in the region. In recognition of their gallantry in this historic achievement, Captain Tony Steggles of the Levies received the Military Cross, and Sergeant Mohammed Nakhaira and Lance Corporal Said Salem were awarded the Military Medal. Lt Colonel Johnson, the Commander of the Trucial Oman Levies, received the OBE for his 'distinguished service', which included his role during the Buraimi Operation.

These operations had been carried out by the Levies very close to Fort Jahili and only four years before my arrival, so when I turned up they were still frequently discussed and, coupled with the proximity, I was made even more aware of the recent military activity. Ironically, after all the intrigue and upheaval of the Buraimi Oasis, very probably motivated by the prospect of an oil discovery, nothing of commercial value has ever been found there.

A period of relative calm was restored following the forceful eviction of the Saudis and the removal of four sheikhs who had chosen allegiance to Saudi Arabia rather than to the Sultan.

On 1 March 1956, the name of the Trucial Oman Levies was officially changed to the Trucial Oman Scouts and also from that time the Political Resident was allowed to deploy members of the force outside the borders of the Trucial States. This enabled the TOS to move legally into Omani territory, which became particularly important in July 1957 with the revolt in Oman. This was led by the brothers Ghaleb and Talib bin Ali, and concentrated mainly on laying landmines and ambushes against the Omani military and oil camps. By the end of 1958, the rebels had been cleared from most areas and some 200–300 of them had taken refuge on Jebel Akhdar ('Green Mountain'), so named because of the green plateau close to the highest point. There were only a few narrow tracks up the mountain slope, making the position very easy to defend. Consequently, a decision was taken by the British government to bring in the SAS, whose future at that time was uncertain.

The key to a successful assault was surprise, and C Squadron, along with the Mortar Troop, played an important role in achieving this. These two TOS units were in position at Aqabat on the western side of Jebel Akhdar, from where they engaged the rebels as part of a deception plan. It worked, as many rebels were moved to reinforce their defences since they now believed the imminent assault would come from this direction.

The final assault was made by two SAS squadrons, who reached the summit having first taken out a defensive machine-gun post with a grenade. The rebel leaders managed to escape to Saudi Arabia but most of the rebel tribesmen accepted the offer of amnesty and returned to their homes minus their rifles. It was a victory of immense importance and the part played by the TOS was a significant contributing factor. Sergeant Khamis Hareb received the Military Medal in recognition of his 'gallant and distinguished service' at Aqabat al Dhafra. Sir David Stewart and Sheikh Faisal bin Sultan, to the best of my knowledge, are the only two TOS officers still alive who played an active role in that operation. This successful military action, apart from striking a major blow against the rebels, importantly secured the future of the SAS.

After the stunning and successful assault of Jebel Akhdar, the rebel leaders had scattered, but under the leadership of Talib bin Ali and with financial support from Saudi Arabia they regrouped in early 1959. The rebels' main target continued to be the Sultan of Oman and his forces as well as the oil company. Their main tactics remained the use of landmines and ambushes, which were effective and inflicted heavy casualties on both people and vehicles. The TOS were actively involved in the operation against the rebels and, as we were the resident squadron in that area, both Ian and I were constantly on patrol. Our patrols operated not only in the Buraimi Oasis but also in large areas of Oman. The aim of these patrols was to make life as difficult as possible for the rebels and to cut off the supply of mines and weapons to them.

One of the main smuggling routes for resupplying the rebels with mines and weapons involved camels and donkeys passing through the Trucial States. The Scouts were deployed on tracks that were known to be used and also in more remote areas carrying out stop-and-search checks, which they did with considerable success. Some bright spark, possibly from higher command in Aden, came up with the original idea of bringing in a tracker unit from Kenya. The idea was for them to be located close to the main action areas. The theory was that, on hearing an explosion, they would arrive at the scene as quickly as possible and backtrack the mine-layer's footprints, ideally leading to an arrest. The tracker unit duly arrived, consisting of a handful of the most terrifying African tribesman that any of us had ever seen. They all had initiation scars and extended ear lobes, which they hooked round their ears. Initially, and understandably, our local soldiers would have nothing to do with this wild-looking group. Their leader was a very tall young man named Gilfred Powys, whose family owned one of the biggest cattle ranches in Timau, Kenya. Gilfred was a delightful person and, on arrival, he and his trackers stayed with us at Jahili for a short time to acclimatise and be briefed on the task ahead of them. Although there was no shortage of mine incidents to be investigated, by the time Gilfred and his motley crew arrived on the scene the local people had obliterated all the evidence, deliberately or accidentally who knows. This caused the team great frustration and the word was put out that no one was to go near a mine incident until the trackers arrived. Naturally, this did not work since frequently there were casualties requiring immediate medical attention. Understandably, Gilfred and his gang became so infuriated that on a number of occasions they took their anger out on the 'innocent' bystanders in a physical way. The Kenyans were reported and warned that their actions were not acceptable, but the warnings were not heeded, and eventually the trackers were sent back to Kenya, much to the relief of our soldiers and the civilian population.

My time with B Squadron gave me a good opportunity to improve my Arabic, as I spent a great deal of time patrolling with my Arab soldiers, who rarely spoke a word of English. It was fascinating to see how men from various tribes with a history of friction soldiered together as brothers in arms and rarely allowed their diverse backgrounds to become a serious issue. Attracting recruits to enlist in the TOS was not a problem as there was hardly any other acceptable employment for these proud tribesmen. To be a highly trained soldier with one's own rifle was an honourable profession and many young men were keen to join up.

My soldiers not only helped me with my Arabic but also taught me their customs and culture and, most importantly, how to survive the extreme contrasting changes of climate in the desert. I quickly learned to respect the desert and the dangerous, devastating mood changes that could occur with little notice. I was also taught how our *shemagh* headdress was vital as protection from the sun and sandstorms and how the *agul* (head band), worn to keep the *shemagh* secure on one's head, could also be used to tether one's camel. We were even told that the camel stick that most of us carried could, in desperate times, be forced down the unfortunate beast's throat to make it vomit bile water, which one could drink in preference to dying of thirst. Fortunately, I never had to put the camel stick theory to the test, but it was a close call on one camel patrol – of which more later.

Late in the afternoon of 27 November 1959, Ian and I were out on our balcony at Fort Jahili when there was a huge explosion not too far away, from the direction of Hamasa village. It was obviously a mine, so I quickly collected the guard detail and we rushed off to the scene while Ian organised a larger backup group. Hamasa village was just inside the Omani border, and consisted of the usual *barasti* housing and an old fort. There had been several recent mine incidents in the area, including one involving one of our own three-ton Bedfords. Our only means to limit damage to ourselves from mines was to place sandbags in our vehicles, but this was not very effective, and the extra weight curtailed our ability to travel on sand, especially in the heat of the day. A mysterious intelligence officer had recently arrived who operated on his own and did not answer to our TOS command. He even had a false name (which we saw through in no time at all) and insisted, against our advice, on living on his own in the old Hamasa fort, which was totally isolated and very vulnerable. I can only presume that this strange and dangerous decision was taken in order for him to carry out his clandestine operations unobserved by all of us living in the area.

On arrival at the scene of the explosion, I discovered that the 'anonymous' officer's Land Rover, while being driven by his driver, had hit a mine placed near the entrance to the fort. There was little we could do to help the badly injured driver and, while comforting him as best I could, he died in my arms. It was my introduction to the reality of cold-blooded rebel acts of aggression. It was also a bloody reminder that we were dealing with a formidable group with only one aim: to kill and maim as many of the forces supporting the Sultan as possible.

Shortly after that incident, we received excellent intelligence that resulted in a dawn raid on Hamasa village and the arrest of the suspected mine-layer. True to form, he refused to answer any questions about his involvement in the rebel cause or the location of other mines that we knew had been laid. What could we do? Gradually break his will until eventually he talked, in the meantime accepting further casualties, probably to our own men? Or use methods that one would rather not have to? I am not proud to admit that I used physical pain to speed up this man's recall, but it did result in not only his admission of involvement but also, more importantly, the whereabouts of the other buried mines. As a result of this unconventional but highly effective form of interrogation, we were then able to locate and clear the remaining mines promptly without suffering any further casualties. Torture is literally a sensitive subject, and I completely respect the argument against its use. However, we do not live in a perfect world and, realistically (in my humble opinion), one has to accept that on rare occasions the use of torture can be justified, especially if innocent lives will be saved as a result.

During my time at the fort I was privileged to meet and get to know well HH Sheikh Zayed bin Sultan Al Nahyan, the Ruler's Representative in Al Ain and the brother of HH Sheikh Shakhbut bin Sultan Al Nahyan, the then Ruler of Abu Dhabi. Occasionally in life, one is very fortunate to meet someone and immediately realise that one is in the presence of an exceptional person, and this was certainly the case with Sheikh Zayed. Although he was only of average height and build and modestly dressed, he stood out instantly from all around him. From the first time I was introduced to him I was aware not only of his presence and delightful personality, but also his natural charm, which made one feel relaxed and special in his company. He also deservedly enjoyed massive respect and support from all the people of the area in his capacity of Ruler's Representative. He would sometimes drive into the fort in an open Land Rover, which had seen better days, and would sit with us enjoying a traditional coffee and discussing any problems of mutual concern. He had an intensely inquisitive mind, and was keen to discuss local and world affairs and, in particular, the views of the Western world. We would often talk for hours at a time and our conversation would eventually turn, inevitably, to his love of the history of the region and his passion for his falcons and hunting with them. He always travelled with an entourage that comprised loyal tribesmen, armed with a variety of weapons, and, when visiting him at his home or in the desert, he would also have his magnificent falcons close by. On several occasions I was fortunate to be invited by Sheikh Zayed to go hunting with him and to spend a considerable amount of time in his company. These are very special memories for me, and are constantly in my thoughts. It was so obvious, even then, that here was a great man who loved the desert and everything associated with it, but also more than capable of understanding the complex problems of the modern world. The time would soon arrive when it would be his destiny to transform his beloved desert into what the UAE has become today.

All good things must come to an end, including our time at the desert fort, and it was time for 'Shiny B' to move on. If Fort Jahili was the plum posting (which for me it was), Mirfa undoubtedly had to be the worst. It was a remote tented camp, way out on the coast beyond Abu Dhabi, with intense heat and humidity causing hard living conditions. To get there one had to travel along the coast from Dubai to Abu Dhabi, crossing varying forms of corrugation and treacherous sand that was waiting to cause endless punctures or to bog you down. From the crossroads at Abu Dhabi there was still a journey of another several hours consisting of featureless terrain before reaching the oil company camp at Tarif. This was the location of an American rig that was exploring for oil in the region and one of the reasons for a rifle squadron to be located some 20 miles away. The squadron frequently patrolled the area where the oil company operated. This provided protection for the equipment and, of course, for the oilmen themselves. I think it highly unlikely that the oilmen would have accepted our very basic living conditions, especially since they were provided with the luxury of air-conditioned accommodation, cold beer and fresh rations which were flown in on a regular basis.

Our other duties included patrolling the coastline to search for illegal immigrants looking for work and, although it is difficult to believe, we would occasionally come across pilgrims thinking they were close to the holy city of Mecca. Unscrupulous dhow captains would land these people on the coastline and leave them stranded. They would tell the pilgrims, disorientated and often terrified from their ordeal at sea, that beyond the sand dune in front of them they would find civilisation and all their prayers would be answered. Frequently, our patrols would come across the bodies of those who had sadly perished in their attempt to find work or complete their pilgrimage. Incredibly, only recently, the eldest son of a great friend of mine told me that he had moored his luxury boat at an isolated island and a group of desperate illegal immigrants had approached him for food and water. Had he not visited that island on that day, they too would probably have perished. They informed him that the dhow captain had told them they only had to walk a short distance to reach civilisation. This most recent incident took place more than 50 years after our early days patrolling against similar ruthless human traffickers. It is shocking to know that this still goes on to this day.

One factor that the British officers seconded to the TOS greatly appreciated was the very generous local living allowance, together with the daily ration allowance paid to those of us serving in the outstations. This meant that, while in the outstations, we could exist on our ration allowance and save our monthly salary and local living allowance for the six-week leave to which we were entitled every nine months. This made even the deployment to Mirfa, with its terrible conditions, financially preferable to being in the rifle squadron based in Sharjah, with all its comforts but under the watchful eye of the HQ staff. The Army has never been renowned for its generosity regarding leave, and to get that amount of time off took into account the hardship of our posting and it was accepted that our duties and conditions warranted it.

I had cunningly waited until we were stationed at Mirfa to apply for my first period of UK leave, and during that time I met up with Desmond Cosgrove in London. I remember the two of us wandering around Harrods, gazing in wonder especially at the luxuries in the food department that were denied to us in the Gulf. We also had some fun visiting the travel department, mainly because there was a very pretty girl behind the desk. We told her, trying to keep straight faces, that we were interested in a holiday to a remote location away from the madding crowds and someone had suggested the Trucial States. Not surprisingly, she had never heard of this destination, but after a long search informed us that, according to the little information she could find, she would not recommend it as a holiday resort because the region had little to offer except sand and flies (which was a fairly accurate description).

After my most enjoyable leave, I was soon back to the basic tented life at Mirfa. Flies were extremely frustrating and would appear from nowhere to annoy us even in the most isolated parts of the desert. Some areas, especially over on the Batinah coast, were really badly affected with flies and one needed to cover oneself with a mosquito net while trying to eat. The children, in particular, did not seem to be bothered by flies crawling around their eyes and noses, making little or no effort to brush them away. I could only presume that they had got used to them and put up with them as a normal fact of life. The local people suffered from a great number of eye infections and dysentery in those days, and the flies may well have contributed to that. One of the very few good points about the summer was that, when the heat arrived, the flies disappeared.

After my most enjoyable leave, I was soon back to the basic tented life at Mirfa. I was permanently hot and sweaty, and sleep was only possible for an hour or so at a time. It was sometimes hard to believe that a civilised world existed somewhere out there in the far distance and I often remembered, with a smile, the Harrods girl's fitting description of the Trucial States, and of course her pretty face.

Life for Ian and me was made more bearable by the occasional visit to the oil camp at Tarif for a good meal and a cold beer. We were always made most welcome there and enjoyed the generous hospitality and fresh food. Our soldiers had no such comforts to look forward to and endured the unbearably harsh conditions far better than we did.

One of the favourite pastimes of the oilmen, especially after more than a few beers, was to see who was the champion arm-wrestler. I would always have a go, but used to fail miserably as some of the Americans were really big and strong. Invariably, it was the same huge Texan who would win in the end. Ian was never interested in taking part, but he would watch carefully and whispered to me late one evening at the end of a contest that he thought he could beat the Texan. Having once been on the receiving end of Ian's strength and having witnessed his unbelievable power many times, I had no doubt that he would be capable of taking on the Texan. I threw down the challenge to the Texan, who readily accepted. Ian had incredible strength and could lift a Land Rover in the sand long enough for a punctured tyre to be removed without the assistance of a jack, provided the driver was quick and efficient with the wheel brace. That was no mean feat.

It was agreed that the Texan and Ian would face up to each other on our next visit and I placed the equivalent of a month's pay on Ian to win, without telling him. The great day eventually arrived and off we went for the clash of the Titans. The oilmen had great respect for Ian but the serious money was on their man. Just before the showdown was due to take place, Ian quietly told me he had decided not to go through with it and would withdraw.

'You can't do that,' I selfishly replied. 'I have put a month's wages on you and I will lose it.'

'Very well, my boy, we can't have that, so let's get on with it,' he replied, fortunately for me.

By this time the atmosphere was electric, as the contest had been the main topic of conversation since the challenge had been issued, with drilling activities hardly mentioned.

The two of them took their places, with Ian lighting up a new cigarette and looking as cool as the proverbial cucumber. The Texan immediately applied pressure and Ian's arm took an alarming lurch towards the table surface, which was cheered enthusiastically and loudly by the oilman's many supporters. Ian allowed the Texan to hold him in this perilous position for what seemed ages and then, with a sigh, looked at me and muttered, 'I have had enough of this'. For the first time since the bout had started, Ian looked the Texan straight in the eye. How he did it I do not know, but the Texan's arm was suddenly driven back with such force that, to save it from being broken, he collapsed backwards off his seat and landed on his back on the floor. A deafening silence replaced the oilmen's cheering, followed by their sporting, thunderous congratulations – including from the bewildered Texan himself. Ian had once again entered into the folklore of the TOS and the Gulf. On the way back to camp, with my pockets full of cash, Ian firmly (but with a twinkle in his eye) told me never again to put him in such an embarrassing situation because that would be the last time he would come to the rescue to save my hard-earned wages. I was fortunate to have known and served with many great characters during my time in the Scouts. Some of them were legends, and I have no hesitation in including Ian in that elite group.

During all this time with 'Shiny B', I had never lost sight of my ultimate aim to join an infantry regiment, and I continued to remind both Colonel Carter and Desmond Cosgrove of my ambition at every possible opportunity. One day, without warning, I was summoned to Sharjah and wondered what it was all about. On my arrival, Desmond explained that a contingent from his regiment, the King's Regiment, was coming to Sharjah for some desert training and the CO, Colonel Eric Holt, would be present. Desmond had kindly approached the Colonel on my behalf and he had agreed to meet me.

We met in Desmond's room, away from inquisitive eyes, where I explained that I was desperately keen to stay in the Army, but really only wanted to serve in the infantry. We must have talked for at least a couple of hours, at the end of which Colonel Holt informed me that if Colonel Carter, as my CO, signed my application to transfer from the RASC he would accept me into the King's Regiment. This was the brilliant, exciting news that I had dreamed about, and it was hard to comprehend that it had at last been achieved. True to his word, Colonel Carter immediately signed the necessary form to complete my transfer and it was time to celebrate. The party was on.

When the RASC eventually discovered that my transfer had been approved, they promised that if I stayed I could keep my temporary rank of captain and have a choice of next posting. This was a most tempting offer, but my mind was already made up and I was off to join the King's Regiment. As previously explained, my initial reason for requesting secondment to the TOS had been purely selfish, to try and achieve my ambition to become an infantry officer. However, after the 18 months I had served with the Scouts, I was genuinely grateful for my time there and all the incredible experiences I had had. I knew in my heart that those Arab soldiers and the Gulf States were now very special to me, and would remain so for the rest of my life. There was no way that I could contemplate a future without returning to serve once more with these proud Arab soldiers that I had come to know and respect enormously. The desert sand had entered my blood and I had no doubt that it would remain there. Similarly, I would never take for granted the parts played by Colonels Carter and Holt, plus my old friend Desmond Cosgrove, for making my dream of becoming an infantry officer a reality and I will always appreciate their support and encouragement.

It was a case of crying in one eye and smiling in the other when I departed from Sharjah. There was sadness that I was leaving a military life and special force that now meant so much to me, but also excitement about my future as an infantry officer in a regiment with so much history and tradition. It would be another five full and exciting years before I would return to the people and the desert that remained constantly in my thoughts.

BERLIN, THE BEATLES AND JOHN F KENNEDY

Before achieving my long-held dream of joining an infantry regiment, I first had to visit the regimental tailor in London to be measured up and fitted for my new King's Regiment uniforms. The clothing allowance I received fell way short of the horrendous tailor's bill but, fortunately, I had saved more than enough from my time in the TOS to cover it. Then it was off to the infantry training establishments at Hythe and Warminster to learn my new trade as an infantry officer. I was determined to work hard in order to achieve the highest possible grades to prove to Colonel Holt that his faith in me had been justified. Fortunately, I managed to do this on both courses and towards the end of 1961, with a feeling of nervous excitement, flew to Nairobi, Kenya, where the battalion was stationed.

I became a platoon commander and quickly developed a good relationship both with the Kingsmen in my platoon and with my brother officers. The Kingsmen, many of whom were National Servicemen, mainly hailed from Manchester and Liverpool and had a vocabulary of their own which we knew as 'The King's English'. Suffice to say I loved my regiment, I loved the tough, rigorous demands of being an infantry officer and I loved the beauty of Kenya.

Being in Kenya also gave me the opportunity to meet up again with Gilfred Powys. We had last met in the Trucial States where he had been the leader of the tracking unit that had been sent back to Kenya at short notice. He kindly invited my platoon to spend a week training on the family ranch at Timau, which I was delighted to accept, much to the envy of the others. One of the highlights, after giving my men a lecture on camouflage concealment from the air, was to take up Gilfred's offer of a flight in his single-engine plane to check out the trenches from above. On nearing the platoon's position, Gilfred deliberately idled the engine. Then, with great enthusiasm, we hurled paper bags filled with very smelly cattle dung and thunder flashes onto the unsuspecting men below. My platoon, and their noses, had learned the need for better concealment from above. When we landed, I was horrified to learn that Gilfred had only acquired the plane a few days earlier and had not had any flying lessons!

All too soon, it was time to sail from Mombasa. Many of us were leaving with wonderful memories of the African continent, and there were more than a few broken hearts.

For a few months in 1962 we were stationed in the magnificent city of Chester, before being on the move again, this time to Berlin. Very soon after arrival, everyone was taken on a tour to witness at first hand the incredible contrast between the drab buildings and obvious poverty in the east of the divided city and the affluent lifestyle enjoyed in the west. We were also briefed that we should treat all Berliners with great caution, and presume that one third of them were spies, another third were potential spies and the remaining third retired spies. This was to become an even more fascinating (albeit tongue-in-cheek) statistic for me when, shortly after our arrival in Berlin, I was sent to Maresfield in England to attend an intensive intelligence course. This course concentrated mainly on the activities and equipment of the Soviet forces, which knowledge would enable us to identify their different military units. We were also informed that, despite all efforts to conceal our personal military details, the KGB would obtain them and open a file on each of us. To our dismay, we were also told that our files would be regularly updated throughout our military service. Comrade Brother was watching us!

Part of my duties on my return to Berlin was to cross through Checkpoint Charlie into East Berlin on a regular basis to carry out reconnaissance tasks known as 'Flag Flying'. One of the main aims of this was to observe any military movements and, importantly, to be seen by East Berliners. Normally, once the inhabitants realised that we were from the West, they would look around carefully and, if there was no sign of East German or Soviet forces, wave nervously to us. I have always thought the saying 'communist with knife and fork wishes to meet communist with steak and kidney pie' an accurate assessment of that political movement.

Probably my most terrifying experience was to be nominated Parade Adjutant for the Queen's Birthday Parade in Berlin. This was a grand ceremonial parade composed of three infantry regiments, and probably second in size only to Trooping the Colour on Horse Guards Parade in London attended by Her Majesty each year. This particular year, the Berlin parade was to be televised all over Europe and would be attended by many thousands of enthusiastic spectators. The problem was that, as the Parade Adjutant, I would be one of three officers on parade mounted on German police horses. The only previous contact I had ever had with horses was the occasional flutter on one, usually with no success. As the most junior of the mounted officers, there is no prize for guessing who finished up with the meanest beast, ears constantly pinned back and a mind of his own. I also suspected from the start that he was probably anti-British for good measure. In rehearsals I spent more time falling off the horse than sitting on it, much to the amusement of Herr Schneider, the dour German police horse trainer. Herr Schneider was not my favourite person and every time I complained about the horse's refusal to comply with my orders he would mount the horse, which would then behave in an exemplary manner. Come the big day, I was completely terrified that the horse and I would part company, with the moment captured on television and witnessed by the huge crowd and all present on parade. When it was time to meet up with my unpredictable mount and lead the parade onto the parade ground, I hardly recognised it. Herr Schneider had exercised the wretched animal so hard early that morning that it could hardly walk, let alone gallop, and, to my eternal relief, we both came through the ordeal with me still firmly in the saddle. After the undoubted success of the parade, Herr Schneider became my close friend and we laughed about painful, embarrassing experiences as we celebrated in great style till the wee hours. The next day, I passed by the stables to share a carrot with my new four-legged best friend, and was convinced that he gave me a wink when I left him, but sadly I could not see too well because of a sudden and inexplicable watering of my eyes.

Being stationed in Berlin, divided up between the Americans, French, Russians and ourselves, was a strange experience, especially for the Berliners. We frequently carried out joint exercises with the other Western units to prepare for a Soviet invasion. Fortunately, our intelligence reports indicated that such an invasion was not being planned for the near future, as our combined military presence would not have offered much resistance to the Red Army.

However, we all thought this might change after the visit to West Berlin by President John F Kennedy in June 1963. The president began his tour with a visit to Checkpoint Charlie, accompanied by the popular Mayor of Berlin, Willy Brandt, before moving on to the front of the Rathaus Schöneberg in Rudolph-Wilde-Platz. Here, in what is regarded as one of his finest speeches, he told a wildly enthusiastic crowd of several hundred thousand West Berliners that he challenged the oppression of the communist world and that the people of West Berlin represented the free world. He went on to say not only that he was very proud of them, but also 'Ich bin ein Berliner'. By all accounts, this emotional, powerful message was greeted with a deafening roar of approval by all those fortunate enough to have been there and hear his inspiring words.

President Kennedy had earlier arrived in the French sector at Tegel airport, where a joint French, American and British force along with a German police unit formed a military reception for him. The King's Regiment represented the British forces, and Desmond Cosgrove and I were selected for the historic occasion – a far cry from our desert past. I was also proudly carrying our Regimental Colour, a very special honour. As is normally the case with these multinational military events, there was a great deal of wrangling, mainly between the American and French authorities, to decide the format for the parade. The Americans insisted that their contingent should be in the place of honour on the right of the parade because it was for an American president. The French refused this demand, pointing out that Tegel airport was in the French sector and arguing that it was therefore correct for them to be on the right. As usual, the French not only won the argument but also insisted that the parade commander would be a Frenchman and give all the words of command in French. This required urgent French lessons for our confused Kingsmen and our furious American counterparts, with only the German police detachment happy to go along with everything since initially they were not going to be represented at all.

The historic day arrived and, when Air Force One was still just a speck in the sky, the French commander called us to attention. This meant no physical movement was allowed for ages, until the plane finally landed. The long time spent at attention was bad enough for all on parade, but for me – having to control our heavy Regimental Colour in a gusty wind – it was agonising. My thoughts towards the French commander became less than fraternal the longer we remained at attention. Fortunately, all went well and the moment that President

Kennedy stopped in front of me and respectfully bowed his head to acknowledge the Regimental Colour is another moment that will live with me forever.

Only five months after his triumphant visit to West Berlin came the devastating news of his assassination. I still vividly remember taking part in the huge candlelit procession that slowly made its way to the place where he had made his historic speech. Here the same crowd that had been so visibly moved by this dynamic young world leader, who had offered them so much hope, held an all-night vigil, and there and then renamed the square John-F. Kennedy-Platz. This was undoubtedly a very moving and sad time throughout the world and, in West Berlin especially, there was an overwhelming feeling of great sadness.

The Spandau Prison Guard was another demanding but unforgettable duty. Berlin-based forces of all the WW2 allies, including the Russians, took turns for a month at a time to guard the infamous prisoners. Signing for the safe custody of three of Hitler's most well-known war criminals (Hess, Speer and von Shirach) for 24 hours was quite a nerve-racking responsibility and to see the three of them in their overalls, relaxing or working in their garden, was a remarkable experience. Hess, of course was the best known of the three and to this day his solo flight into Scotland, allegedly in an attempt to negotiate peace with the United Kingdom, remains something of a mystery. As the officer in charge of the external security of the prison, I was able to watch the men in the prison garden and I always exchanged courteous greetings in German with them, but only from a safe distance. This was a precaution in case one or all of them attempted to overpower me and take possession of my service revolver, which would not have done my military career any favours. The fact that Hess was also known to be suicidal was another good reason for keeping one's distance. In 1987, when he was the only remaining prisoner in Spandau (mainly because of the Soviet refusal to consider his release), he apparently committed suicide at the age of 93. I am glad I never lost any of these notorious prisoners during my numerous 24-hour prison duties; just as well, as it would have probably resulted in a court martial followed by a firing squad.

West Berlin was an exciting city. We worked hard and, when we could afford it, we played hard as well, with an abundance of delightful young *Fräuleins,* who were only too happy to be escorted by dashing, gallant young British officers.

The nightlife was incredible, and an evening spent visiting nightclubs with Harry Secombe and Stanley Baker lived up to this justified reputation. They had both taken part in a mainly Welsh variety show to entertain the troops, which was followed by a reception for all the visiting artists. Somehow, I finished up with these two Welshmen, who made it quite clear that they wanted a good night out to sample the West Berlin nightlife and I was to be their guide. We visited many of the famous clubs but, as the night progressed, we eventually found ourselves in a nightclub of dubious repute. We were soon surrounded by charming hostesses with an amazing appetite for the expensive drinks that my new, generous Welsh friends were more than happy to pay for, and a good time was being had by all. However, this did not last as, quite abruptly, Stanley Baker, with a look of disbelief and horror on his face, informed us that he had just discovered that his 'companion,' with whom he had been having a cosy chat, needed a shave. This sent Harry Secombe rolling on the ground hysterically, and it was only after they hurriedly paid the bill and we abruptly left the premises that Stanley Baker began, reluctantly, to see the funny side of it. This did not prevent him from threatening us both with every possible torture known to mankind if we ever repeated the embarrassing incident to anyone. Sadly, they have both departed this world and only now am I brave enough to repeat it publicly.

One of my other duties as Intelligence Officer was to look after the public relations for the regiment. National Service was coming to an end and our new CO, a red-headed, fiery Scotsman by the name of McDonald, repeatedly reminded me of the importance of obtaining good press coverage back home to attract potential recruits. The longer I came up with nothing for the press, the more irate he became, and he kept demanding to know when I would rectify this.

I had read in a newspaper that a musical group called the Beatles were attracting a great deal of publicity and were scheduled to appear soon at the Olympia Theatre in Paris. This sent my idle brain into overdrive. The thought of persuading this up-and-coming Liverpool group to come to West Berlin and put on a show for their fellow Liverpudlians was an exciting one. The publicity, I presumed, would be beneficial for all of us and, importantly, it would get the Colonel off my back. Somehow, I managed to make contact with their publicity representative in Paris, an ex-Royal Navy officer named Brian Sommerville. He politely informed me that the intense schedule already in place for the Fab Four during their short stay in Paris would not allow time for a trip to Berlin. He did, however, express his willingness to assist should I come up with another suggestion.

I hit on the idea of having the entire battalion on the parade square to form up in a single line and, starting with the CO, sign a petition asking the Beatles to come and entertain us. This was duly done, having tipped off the press in advance about the 'Petition Parade' that was going to take place. This would, I hoped, ensure a well-publicised story plus some follow-up and a response from the Beatles. Once the deed was done, I informed Brian Sommerville of my cunning scheme, but this did not amuse him at all, although we did work out a compromise. Kingsman Packham, a member of the Regimental Band, and I would travel to Paris to meet the four lads and hand over the petition, which would ensure that all of us involved would receive maximum publicity from the occasion. This duly happened, which is how I came to spend a weekend at the Hotel George V in Paris as a guest of the Beatles, and travel with them in their Rolls-Royce from the hotel to the theatre to watch them in action.

On arrival at the world-famous hotel, we were told that our rooms were ready and that we just had to sign for everything, as we were the personal guests of the Beatles. This was an enormous relief, as I doubted that my month's salary would begin to cover the cost of even one night's accommodation at this five-star hotel. Before the press conference and handing over the petition, Brian Sommerville introduced Kingsman Packham and me to the Fab Four. They could not have made us more welcome and, incredibly, all four of them called me 'Sir' when I shook their hands. The initial thought that struck me was that they were very decent young lads with no airs or graces, and actually very similar to the young Liverpudlians we had serving in the Regiment. It was explained to the press that, as much as they would love to come to Berlin and entertain the troops, their tight schedule would not permit it. Then, to my surprise, they informed the gathering that after the evening's two shows they would make a special broadcast for all the servicemen in Germany. To my utter delight, I was asked to travel with them in the Rolls from the hotel to the Olympia Theatre, during which time I finally managed to persuade them to call me David. I also remember Ringo looking out at a gendarme on traffic duty complete with traditional cloak, commenting that he looked just like Captain Marvel!

Before our arrival at the theatre, the lads told me there would probably be a few, mainly female, fans waiting for them and that I should stay as close as possible to them when we got out of the car and ran for the safety of the stage door. The 'few' turned out to be several hundred adoring, screaming young ladies and, by the time we had run the gauntlet, chunks of my hair had been pulled out and all my regimental blazer buttons ripped off, much to the amusement of the four of them. I have often wondered how those now elderly ladies who were there that day explain to their no doubt jealous friends how the fair hair (probably grey by now) in their possession came from the distinctive black hairstyle made famous by the Beatles.

The first half of the show at the Olympia was performed by Trini Lopez of *If I Had a Hammer* fame. Then it was time for Les Beatles. Until then I had not really taken much interest in their music, but from that moment, and seeing them live from the best seat in the house, I was totally overwhelmed. It comes as no surprise to me that, to this day, their music is still so popular and recognised, and even enjoyed, by my grandchildren's generation.

I sat through both performances, during which they had the audience going wild with excitement and screaming for more before they eventually took their final bow. On finding my way backstage, I congratulated them and joined them in a few whisky-and-lemonades, which they consumed at a fair rate, before making our broadcast to the troops in Germany. I joined in the question-and-answer session and they all contributed a special message to our battalion in Berlin, which also included an apology for not having time to visit. Interestingly, they were then asked to do an interview for Russian listeners, and I vividly recall Paul telling the others to take this seriously. He explained that the Russians might not understand any ad hoc light-hearted remarks and this could lead to unnecessary negative publicity. At that time Paul was definitely the leader of the group.

On our return to the hotel, I told them that I intended to make the most of my night in Paris and, as they had no further engagements, I asked if they would like to join me. All of them said they would love to but, because of their incredible popularity, it would be impossible to appear in public without the press and their adoring fans having a field day and ruining the night out. At lunchtime the next day, as promised, I joined them to bid them farewell and thank them for their kindness and the support they had given. They could not wait to ask me how I had got on the night before and whether I had been lucky enough to meet a friendly, obliging, young French lady. It was then that I realised it was all very well to have fame and fortune, but it also meant giving up the freedom of a normal life which we lesser mortals take for granted. In reality they were prisoners, albeit in very comfortable cells, confined to a life of constant glare and scrutiny from the media and the general public, from which there was no escape. I do look back on that Paris encounter with great affection and have been told by my family and friends that I have been known to bring up my time with the Beatles far too frequently. Yeah, Yeah, Yeah.

One evening, at a regimental dinner night, and dressed in formal Mess kit, I was called out at short notice to rush into East Berlin via our official crossing point at Checkpoint Charlie. I was hurriedly briefed that a report had been received stating that a large movement of military vehicles was taking place, and I was to investigate. There was no time to change my uniform so, with my driver (who fortunately was sober, unlike me, having partaken of a glass or two) I entered the Soviet sector. We soon heard the sound of heavy vehicles and discovered that convoy after convoy of lorries and tank transporters were on the move. Telling my driver to remain vigilant and to keep an eye on me, I walked across the road to take a closer look. I must have looked like a well-illuminated Christmas tree in my red Mess kit, and within seconds I had attracted the attention of a group of East German police. First they surrounded me, then blocked my way forward and began forcibly pushing me back in the direction of my staff car. Our Berlin Regulations made it very clear that at no time in the Soviet sector were we to recognise or enter into dialogue with East German police or military, but should demand that they call a Russian officer. When confronted by these East German policeman, I defiantly (and probably pompously, after imbibing of a fair amount of port at the dinner night) demanded that a Russian officer be sent for. This request was ignored but I stood my ground, refusing to be pushed further. They then became very aggressive and, despite my determined resistance, I was eventually knocked to the ground and a game of football started, with me as the ball. My driver must have witnessed all this from the car, and he somehow managed to mount the kerb and drove at the policemen, scattering them in all directions. He then helped me back into the car and we made our way as quickly as possible back to the safety of West Berlin.

We went straight to our Military Headquarters, where I reported the incident to a senior intelligence staff officer who had been called from his bed to hear my story. Eventually, I was allowed to be patched up at the Military Hospital, but my expensive Mess jacket was ruined. I was told by my CO that Her Majesty's Government would demand an apology for the brutal assault on a British officer, but I never heard of any such demand being made. Some wag suggested that the incident had been diplomatically dropped, rather than provide possible justification for starting World War Three. (If so, I would have been somewhat disappointed not to be regarded of sufficient importance to warrant going to war over. I felt the very least they could have done was to reimburse me the cost of replacing my very expensive Mess jacket, which would have been considerably cheaper than any military intervention, but this too was denied!)

On another occasion, a few of us had gone to the well-known Resi Bar, famous for its water music display and its unique method of sending messages to other tables via a cylindrical tube system. It was always fun to send word by these means to tables occupied by pretty young ladies inviting them to join us, and see the reaction when the message arrived at their table. On this particular evening, we were still looking for a suitable table to send our invitation to when we, for a change, were the recipients of a message inviting us for a drink. Our delight was short-lived when we saw that it was a lone man who had sent the message, but a free drink was always acceptable, as we were nearly always broke. We had a couple of drinks with the hospitable German, who said it was an honour to meet serving British officers, but we left as soon as his offer of free drinks dried up, in search of more attractive (and feminine) company. A couple of days later, the secure, ex-directory telephone in my intelligence office rang, and to my astonishment the caller introduced himself as the man we had met at the Resi Bar. He laughed when I demanded to know how he had obtained my number, and alarmingly added that he knew plenty more about me. He invited me to join him at the weekend at a well-known restaurant, saying that he had an attractive proposal to put to me. I accepted and agreed to meet him the following Saturday, then immediately went and reported the conversation to the Brigade Intelligence Officer. He agreed that I had done the right thing and that I should meet with my mysterious caller as arranged.

Sure enough, when I arrived at the restaurant our man from the Resi Bar was sitting at a table waiting for me. Over lunch he explained to me that he was part of small group dedicated to bringing deserving people who were in danger of arrest in East Berlin to safety in the West, and that he needed my help. He told me about a young female student who had been accused of anti-communist propaganda and would be detained in the very near future. He explained in graphic detail how, following her imminent arrest, she would be interrogated and tortured by the dreaded Stasi, the hated and feared East German state security service with close links to the Russian KGB. Incredibly, he was aware that I frequently went 'flag flying' to East Berlin. He went on to explain that he could organise for the girl to be put in the boot of my car at a discreet location on my next trip. It would then be possible to bring her safely over the border to the West, via Checkpoint Charlie, as he knew it was forbidden for the East German border police to stop and search our military vehicles. I told him that I would think it over and contact him at the number he gave me, but that the attractive offer of money he also mentioned would not be necessary. I made it very clear to him that there was no question of my being involved for financial gain. Besides, who was I to decline the opportunity to become a knight in shining armour and, mounted on my white horse, come to the rescue of a fair lady in distress.

As planned, I reported back to Brigade HQ, who promptly informed me that they were aware of my recent conversation, as they had placed some of their own people at the restaurant complete with a listening device. Feeling more and more like the great James Bond himself, I was ordered not to discuss the matter with anyone and not to make any further contact with my shadowy Berliner. It later transpired that the whole thing was an elaborate East German attempt to try and persuade a British officer to smuggle a girl into the West and be caught in the process. This would have resulted in an extremely embarrassing international incident, with the distinct possibility of my being jailed in East Germany on a kidnap charge. For the record, I never heard from the man again and my ex-directory telephone number was rapidly changed. It is only now, safe in the knowledge that the Berlin Wall is no more, and Germany is once more united, that I feel comfortable telling this story.

After two fascinating years, we left Berlin at the end of 1964 and the Battalion headed for Ballykinlar in Northern Ireland. All too soon, we discovered that the locals were not nearly as friendly as the Berliners and we were forbidden from leaving the barracks in uniform unless on duty. The verbal and physical abuse to which we were occasionally subjected was most unpleasant, especially as we were not allowed to retaliate. Not too long after our arrival, however, I was informed that I was to be posted to the Brigade Depot at Fulwood Barracks, Preston, as the second-in-command of the Training Company. This was not something I could get excited about and I did not relish the thought of leaving the regimental life that I thoroughly enjoyed, not forgetting my brother officers and the Kingsmen with whom I had been privileged to serve. In my new role I had no option but to settle down and focus on the important task of turning raw basic recruits into trained soldiers, capable of joining their battalions after roughly 12 weeks.

It was soon after this posting that that I decided to apply to rejoin the TOS. The thought of spending at least two years mainly sitting behind a desk planning training programmes and dealing with recruits, who far too frequently had family and personal problems, did not appeal to me at all. My application was turned down, with the comment that I should accept that I was not Lawrence of Arabia and should concentrate on 'proper soldiering'.

At much the same time, I met a young lady who was a well-known actress in the TV soap, Coronation Street, and our relationship blossomed. Frequently, when time permitted, I would travel to Manchester to wait for her at a pub close to the Granada studios. Over a pint or two I met many TV personalities, including Michael Parkinson, and enjoyed their company and their refreshing outlook on life. From the age of 18 I had known only military life and the hard discipline associated with it, and it was a new and enjoyable experience to be in the company of free-thinking individuals. I also came to the conclusion that, if I could not return to the soldiering I had experienced in the TOS, I would have to think very carefully about my military career, as the prospect of postings in the UK and Germany left me cold. Over a beer I talked about my predicament to many of the Granada staff and, somewhere along the line, I was persuaded to write to Granada requesting an interview to be taken on as a newsreader or something similar. To my surprise, and no doubt with more than a little help from my pub mates and girlfriend, I was invited to attend an interview, which would also include a screen test. It was an even greater surprise that, following the interview – which included a mock reading of the news and interviewing a 'celebrity' – that I received a letter from Granada TV offering me a vacancy with the daily news programme *Scene at Six Thirty*. This popular programme was competently led by no less than Parkinson himself and was the start of his highly successful career as a popular TV personality.

Now I really was in a predicament. Should I take the plunge into the unknown and quit soldiering, which I loved, or should I try, once more, to return to the TOS? I requested a meeting with my CO and informed him as diplomatically as possible that if I was not considered for the Scouts again I would reluctantly resign my commission and take up an offer in the world of television. No one, and certainly not a junior officer, can hold Her Majesty's Forces to ransom and it was not my intention to do so. However, I was being totally honest. Shortly after this discussion, the Colonel called me in to inform me that a vacancy would arise in a few months for a new commander of the Support Group with the TOS. It had been agreed that, provided I passed the Support Weapons course with a good report, the position would be mine. It took me no time at all to take the decision to soldier on, and off I went to the Support Weapons School at Netheravon to learn all about the latest weapons, including the 81 mm mortar that the TOS Support Group had recently acquired. I passed the course with a top grade and, with that, I was on my way back to Sharjah. The only difference was that this time I knew what to expect and I could not wait to get there.

I have never regretted the decision not to join Granada TV but, from time to time, have wondered what would have happened to me if I had gone there. I will never know, and Michael Parkinson never had to look over his shoulder for a possible rival. Only joking, Parky!

'THREE INCH'

On my return to the Trucial States I did not go directly to the TOS HQ in Sharjah but instead to Aden to attend an Arabic language course. At that time (1966) Aden had to be one of the most godforsaken places in the world, with duty-free shopping one of the few points in its favour. The problem was that, once one had purchased a camera and radio at incredibly low prices, there was not much else to do apart from dodge grenades, ambushes and sniper fire. This happened on a regular basis and is not a recommended healthy outdoor activity.

In 1964, the British Prime Minister, Harold Macmillan, had proposed that Aden and the 15 states of the Federation of Arab Emirates (thereafter called the Federation of South Arabia) should achieve self-government within four years. This resulted in the start of fierce urban terrorism in the area – hardly an ideal environment in which to concentrate on learning Arabic, which is not an easy language to master even in more peaceful surroundings.

The Arabic language school was located within the RAF base at Khormaksar, and it was there that we budding linguists were billeted. Previously, students had been put up at the Crescent Hotel at Steamer Point, but a combination of factors (involving expense and having to negotiate 'Murder Mile' on a daily basis) brought to an end the use of that more comfortable living accommodation.

The three-month, highly intensive course was run by an old friend of mine, Owen Taylor, who had previously served in the Scouts. I presumed that I would have a huge advantage over the others on the course with my knowledge of basic army Arabic from my earlier time with the Scouts, but this was not the case. The language school concentrated on teaching us correct grammatical language and vocabulary, so for me it was 'out with the old and in with the new'. I thoroughly enjoyed the course and passed comfortably, which was rewarded with a cash lump sum plus a daily linguist's allowance. My only regret was that I concentrated too much on the spoken word and, as a result, never mastered the written word. At the time I did not think this was too serious, as the vast majority of our soldiers were illiterate. However, to this day I wish I had mastered both, and I realise now that, just as with my school days, I should have worked harder.

After five turbulent and eventful years away from the Middle East, apart from the Arabic course, I once more stepped off an RAF plane into the heat of Sharjah. My first impression was that it did not appear that much had changed, which was confirmed by the journey to our wonderful old Officers' Mess located on the seashore. Upon my arrival, I was greeted by all the old staff, including the newly promoted Staff Sgt Iqbal. It really felt like coming home and, when Gus appeared with that memorable grin that would light up the darkest sky, I knew I was back where I belonged. I recall that, when Gus and I had made our emotional farewells to each other on my departure five years earlier, I solemnly swore to him that I would return one day and Gus told me he would be there waiting for me. In all the time that I had been away, he had refused to look after any other officer and had worked as a waiter or helped out in the kitchen. I soon discovered, however, that his time in the kitchen had unfortunately done nothing to improve his culinary skills. There was only one person I knew who was actually a worse cook than Gus and, as that happened to be me, I had no option but to resign myself to his usually burnt offerings. Thanks to the temperamental kerosene fridge, which still refused to keep anything remotely cool, I managed to survive on a diet consisting mainly of tins of corned beef and pilchards, which even Gus had difficulty in ruining, though he did get close on numerous occasions.

Little may have changed in terms of scenery or buildings in Sharjah and the surrounding areas, but there had recently been very significant political changes.

There had been a wave of support for Arab nationalism in the Middle East, with Gamal Abdel Nasser being recognised as the popular and charismatic leader of the Arab Nationalist Movement.

The radio station *Sawt al Arab*, located in Cairo, had a large and attentive audience. Much of its propaganda was targeted at British colonial dominance of the Trucial States, with regular criticism of the lack of development due to insufficient funding from Britain. Internally, as more Emiratis started to attend the schools that were beginning to open, some of the younger generation were beginning to question the wisdom of the traditional rulers and to debate the merits of a more democratic form of government. Iraq was also becoming increasingly vocal, adding its voice to propaganda accusing the British government of a policy that allowed for mass immigration from Iran to the Gulf States to counter the growing demand for liberation.

In October 1964, a delegation from the Arab League had visited not only all seven Trucial States but also Bahrain and Qatar, promising the poorer states much-needed financial assistance to improve the living conditions of their people. Understandably, this was well received, especially in Sharjah and Ras Al Khaimah, whose rulers were increasingly becoming frustrated at not being able to do more for their subjects. Abu Dhabi, on the other hand, was receiving enormous revenue from oil, but the Ruler, Sheikh Shakhbut, was extremely frugal in helping out the other states and even in his own state there were rumblings of discontent. Many of his subjects were becoming more and more outspoken, as there was little sign of the development that they had expected from the vast income now being received.

The British government became even more alarmed when there was talk by the Arab League of opening offices in the Trucial States, and once again Sharjah and Ras Al Khaimah were mentioned. Any permanent presence of the Arab League in the Trucial States was seen by the Foreign Office as a serious threat to Britain's role in the Gulf and the British government made it clear that it would take drastic steps if necessary to prevent this from happening.

Not for the first time, the Foreign Office believed that the most suitable solution to such a problem would be a financial incentive, and this message was relayed through Sir William Luce, the Political Resident in Bahrain. The British proposal to counter the promise from the Arab League was to make money available to the Gulf rulers, and an agreement was reached to create the Trucial

States Development Fund (TSDF). The British government hoped that funding for this would come not only from the Foreign Office but also from the more wealthy states such as Abu Dhabi and Bahrain. An approach for contributions was also made to Kuwait and Saudi Arabia. Somewhat tongue-in-cheek, the British also invited the Arab League to participate financially. However, the British made it abundantly clear that any funds received would be managed by the TSDF on its behalf. Not surprisingly, this offer was firmly rejected by the Arab League.

Money for the new fund was proving to be difficult to raise, as some of the wealthier Arab countries were being pressurized by the Arab League to make any contribution to the Trucial States through the League itself. At the same time, it was apparent that the British government was reluctant to provide the financial resources needed to implement development programmes on its own. In May 1965, Dr Sayed Nofal, Deputy Secretary-General of the Arab League, arrived in the Trucial States at short notice and visited the rulers of the six northern states. His main mission was to try to obtain their agreement to accept funding directly from the Arab League. The League even went as far as outlining individual development projects for each state. Only Dubai declined the offer of direct financial assistance. Sharjah and Ras Al Khaimah agreed to the Arab League opening offices in their states. This was acutely embarrassing for the Foreign Office, which had only secured about one third of the £900,000 Nofal was claiming to have at his disposal. Nofal's visit coincided with the appearance of George Thomson, Minister of State at the Foreign Office. He immediately confronted each of the five rulers who in principle had accepted aid from the Arab League. From the records of the five meetings with Thomson, Sheikh Saqr bin Sultan Al Qasimi of Sharjah appeared to be the most defiant, but Thomson noted that Sheikh Saqr bin Mohammed Al Qasimi of Ras Al Khaimah also confirmed his agreement to allow an Arab League office in his state.

Prime Minister Harold Wilson then pledged the far more substantial sum of £1,000,000 to the TSDF in an attempt to persuade the rulers to ignore the overtures from the Arab League. Despite this financial commitment from the British government, four of the six northern rulers were not impressed. In June 1965, the rulers of Ajman, Ras Al Khaimah, Sharjah and Umm Al Quwain took the joint policy decision to apply for membership of the Arab League and to request their protection. This no doubt caused serious concern and set alarm bells ringing loudly at the Foreign Office. To add to their worries, it was learned that

Fujairah had also been reported to have changed its pro-British stance. If true, this would leave Sheikh Rashid of Dubai feeling very apprehensive, vulnerable and isolated. The British government realised that urgent decisive action was vital to regain the loyalty of the rulers, as there was now a real threat from the Arab League. Unless the British government regained the initiative and resolved the situation, British influence in the region would be lost forever. In a desperate measure, the Foreign Office applied enormous pressure on Saudi Arabia during urgent talks with King Faisal, who was finally persuaded to donate £1,000,000 to the TSDF in an effort to counter the attractive financial offer made by the Arab League.

The Political Agent in Dubai, Glen Balfour Paul, who had worked tirelessly to resolve the situation in Britain's favour, then received a further setback. A meeting was held at his request with all seven rulers to hear his latest news. He happily announced to the rulers that additional funds had been secured from both Britain and Saudi Arabia, which would result in more development projects. Instead of this news being greeted with enthusiasm, however, he was surprised to see that there was only tacit acknowledgement of the new projects offered. The rulers of Sharjah and Ras Al Khaimah, in particular, advised him that they still intended to approve the opening of Arab League offices in their states and to accept the proposed development projects offered by them. The British now had to deal with an unprecedented dilemma as the new financial offer had failed to convince all of the rulers to 'toe the line'. This left them with very little up their sleeve in the way of new incentives to negotiate with, except the authority to ban non-Trucial State subjects from entering the Gulf by refusing them entry visas.

The use of the TOS to forcibly remove political figures who had entered illegally was discussed by the British authorities and it was agreed that such action could only be taken if it could be carried out in such a way as not to create public outrage. This was recognised by Balfour Paul as a further sign of weakness, and both he and the Political Resident in Bahrain strongly argued the case for firm positive action. Britain's response was to close down the major international airports operating in the Trucial States for 'urgent repair works' on 16 June 1965.

On 22 June, the Foreign Office was informed that a delegation of the Arab League would visit the Trucial States on the 25th. They would be travelling on passports issued by Sharjah, thereby eliminating the need to procure a visa. Records of the events of the two days leading up to 24 June are still not available to the public at the National Archives, but it is known that on that morning Sheikh Saqr bin Sultan Al Qasimi, the Ruler of Sharjah, was summoned to the Political Agency in Dubai. He was informed that, at the request of the ruling family, he was to be replaced by Sheikh Khalid bin Mohammed. Sheikh Saqr bin Sultan was then immediately flown to Bahrain courtesy of the Royal Air Force, which had been instructed to have an aircraft on standby in readiness to remove the Sharjah ruler once he had been made aware of the decision.

The official line from the British government stressed that this action was not politically motivated and had been taken only after a request had been made by the family to replace him. However, this explanation was hardly plausible and I do not believe the services of Sherlock Holmes would be required to understand the real reason for deposing the ruler and the dominant role played by the British government in this action. In the days following the removal of Sheikh Saqr bin Sultan, the main British priority was to communicate with the other rulers in an attempt to divert them from further liaison with the Arab League. This decisive action was also intended to bring the other wavering rulers back into line and to cooperate fully with the British government once again.

On 30 June, a further meeting was held, attended by five rulers with Sheikh Zayed representing Abu Dhabi and Sheikh Khalid of Ras Al Khaimah standing in for his father Sheikh Saqr bin Mohammed Al Qasimi. Thanks to further contributions from the UK and Saudi Arabia, the TSDF now had some £2,500,000 at its disposal. Following recent events and the improved financial funding, the attendees agreed unanimously to implement the development projects that had already been discussed once funds became available. With the removal of the ruler of Sharjah, and the substantial amounts now in the TSDF, the British government had finally regained the upper hand from the Arab League, but it had been a close call.

There were many new faces in the Scouts when I arrived back in early 1966. Fortunately, some of the old and bold were still around to provide much-needed continuity and this made it a lot easier for me to settle in again. The legendary Colonel Carter had gone, and Colonel Freddie de Butts was now firmly in charge. He had a completely different, more reserved personality but had managed to gain the respect of all in the force and was very popular. A fifth squadron, X squadron, had been formed and was commanded by long serving Scout officer

Ken Wilson.It would be hard to accept that X, the cross of St Andrew and Ken, a passionate Scot, are all purely coincidental and no doubt Ken was successful in the naming of his squadron. Ken loved a good argument, especially late at night with a bottle of scotch to loosen the tongue, and frequently would change his views on a subject from one night to the next. I will never forget the two of us attending Colonel Carter's wedding in London, attired in our hired Moss Bros morning suits with Ken trying desperately to keep on his head a grey 'topper' which was far too small for him. (Needless to say, the hat did not make it back to Moss Bros the next day.) He was a great soldier who loved the TOS and all it proudly stood for. Ken would have been a fish out of water serving anywhere else, which was why he was sensibly allowed to remain with the Scouts from 1957 to 1975. No doubt his proudest moment was when he was promoted to command the newly formed Union Defence Force (UDF) for a year or so in 1974. He finally retired and returned to Scotland, where he sadly died of cancer a few years later. I most certainly will never forget him.

It took a couple of days to get kitted out and brought up to date with the ever-changing political upheavals. My intelligence briefing concentrated mainly on the emergence of the threat from the Arab League and the change of ruler in Sharjah. With these formalities concluded, I was off to Manama, a two-hour drive inland, to join my new command, Support Group. Just as B Squadron was affectionately known as 'Shiny B,' the Support Group was always known as 'Three Inch', a reference to the old three-inch mortar even though it had now been replaced by the more sophisticated 81 mm version.

Support Group was a wonderful command to have and Robert Bewell, from whom I took over, had done an excellent job, which ensured that the handover went smoothly. Not only did we have the 81 mm mortars and Browning machine guns, but we were also equipped with Dodge Power Wagons, which meant we could travel to the really remote areas which even the trusty, reliable Land Rover could not reach. As if this wasn't enough, I also had a very capable and pleasant British Sergeant by the name of Tom Lamming, who uncomplainingly took over the many administrative and other tasks I unfairly placed on his broad shoulders.

Support Group was very much a law unto itself and, provided we kept a low profile and submitted monthly training programmes (which I doubt anyone ever looked at), we were left to our own devices. Initially, I lived at the Training Squadron Officers' Mess, which was located close by, complete with electricity and air conditioning. This most welcome modern luxury had recently been installed thanks to a newly acquired generator. Despite this improvement, which made life much more bearable, especially in the summer months, I opted for my own basic independent living quarters.

I had my own small *barasti* mess and living accommodation built, in which I was more relaxed even though it meant giving up all the pleasures associated with electricity. It also meant reverting once again to a wretched, useless, unreliable kerosene fridge and a diet consisting of tinned food and warm beer. Most importantly, I now lived at my own campsite and close to my soldiers. It also meant that I no longer had to listen to the 'heavenly' music played (far too frequently for my ears) by David Goodchild, a delightful Welsh officer. He had somehow managed to bring his harp with him, which had miraculously survived the hazardous journey across the sand dunes.

The Training Squadron commander at the time was Richard Dinnin, a jovial and somewhat eccentric character, who always reminded me of a country squire keeping a paternal eye on all his subjects. Richard was a thoroughly likeable officer and also an excellent artist.

The training base and surrounding facilities were part of the State of Ajman, ruled by another wonderful legend of the Trucial States, HH Sheikh Rashid bin Humaid Al Nuaimi. He had a flowing white beard and was always accompanied by his loyal retinue, who were armed to the teeth. Sheikh Rashid had acceded as Ruler of Ajman in 1928, when the tiny state relied mainly on fishing and the pearl industry for its economic survival. The following year this income collapsed with the introduction of the Japanese cultured pearl. Nevertheless, the young ruler managed to ensure the survival of his impoverished subjects by financing various projects, including the development of agriculture. He never forgot those difficult days and, even with the new-found wealth that came much later to the region, he adopted sensible policies to ensure that all his people benefited from it. He was a true leader, much loved and respected by all, not only in the state of Ajman, but also those, including me, who were fortunate to have known him.

Donkeys had always been allowed to roam the Manama camp freely, albeit with the odd stone aimed at them if they strayed too close to the soldiers' quarters. One particular old donkey used to push his luck, and Richard Dinnin eventually lost his patience and shot the unfortunate beast with his shotgun. Richard presumed this had permanently resolved the problem, until it was discovered that the donkey belonged to the Ruler of Ajman himself. Sheikh Rashid appeared shortly after the shooting incident, accompanied by his well-armed followers. With his flamboyant charm, Richard welcomed the Ruler into the Mess and, in flowing Arabic, greeted him with the traditional 'my home is your home' and invited him to make himself comfortable. After a courteous exchange of pleasantries and coffee, Sheikh Rashid informed Richard that he had heard that one of his donkeys had been shot by him and he would like to see the weapon. Richard obliged and handed over his proud possession to the Ruler, who thanked him and said, with a twinkle in his eye, 'your shotgun is my shotgun'. He then promptly walked out and Richard never saw the weapon again!

On another occasion, I was sitting with HH Sheikh Rashid and asked him why a nearby fort in his territory was abandoned, since it was a magnificent old building. Sheikh Rashid solemnly replied that the fort was haunted and inhabited by evil djinns, and no one would live there. I told him that I had been in the fort many times without encountering any of these evil spirits and, rather than let the fort deteriorate further, he should give it to me. He thought about this for a moment and then replied that, if I spent a night in the fort on my own and came to no harm, the fort would be mine. I accepted the challenge, but must confess it was with considerable apprehension, and against all the advice of my genuinely worried men, that I entered the fort to spend the night alone in the eerie silence. I certainly did not sleep much, frequently waking and attempting to convince myself that nothing untoward was about to happen. Gratefully, I emerged the next morning alive and well, very relieved that I had not encountered any mysterious occupants. After a good breakfast and countless questions from my soldiers, I went to visit Sheikh Rashid to claim my prize. He listened to the story of my uneventful night in the fort and, expressing his surprise, said there had to be a reason why the spirits had not made their presence felt. He suddenly proclaimed that I must have had a bottle of whisky with me for company, which was why the spirits had not come close to me. Despite my honest denial, he refused to believe me and that was the end of it. A pity, really, as I had always wanted to own a fort!

Sheikh Rashid bin Humaid Al Nuaimi was one of the truly great Arab leaders whom I was privileged to meet. I spent many hours in his company, learning a great deal from him of the culture and history of these proud people. I still have amongst my most precious possessions a signed photograph of him and an Ajman stamp album that he presented to me. At a recent TOS reunion in the UAE, I was fortunate to lead a delegation consisting of David Graham and Charles Lumby to pay our respects to his son, the current ruler of Ajman, HH Sheikh Humaid bin Rashid Al Nuaimi. (I had served with Charles in 1960, but only met David for the first time at the reunion as he had joined the UDF in 1974.) During the visit, I was able to recount to the Ruler and all the others present many memories of time spent with his father. Sheikh Humaid particularly enjoyed hearing the stories of the donkey and the fort, which were received with great amusement and laughter.

Support Group was a unique command in many ways. It was commanded by a captain, unlike the five rifle squadrons, which were commanded by majors, and was permanently based in Manama, far from Sharjah and away from the watchful eye of HQ. It was also equipped with the sophisticated new 81 mm mortar, on which no one else was trained. My two Arab officers were Saleh Nasser from Aden and Ahmed Amir, a Dhofari. For good measure I had Karim, a Baluchi quartermaster. Our symbol, which flew proudly from my Land Rover, was a scorpion, which I thought summed us up accurately: small in size but packed with a lethal sting.

Normally, despite the various tribes' geographical and historical differences, the soldiers all worked well together, but in the evenings they would usually congregate in their own tribal groups. I spent a great deal of my spare time sitting with the different ethnic parties over a campfire with coffee and dates, learning their customs and history but making sure never to favour one group over another.

The conversation would often centre on famous events and people of their past. I would frequently be asked about 'London,' which was the only name by which most of the soldiers knew the UK, and about Lawrence and the explorer Thesiger, who was also known as Mubarak bin London. As I began to know my men better, they elaborated more on their beliefs and traditions, including medical remedies that they used. On one occasion, I was persuaded to stand in as goalkeeper in a football match against a rival unit and, while attempting to make a save, I made a desperate dive – to no avail, as the ball still finished in the back of the net. On picking myself up and attempting to ignore the unfavourable remarks about my shortcomings as a goalkeeper, I painfully realised that I had twisted my neck and was in agony. There was no way I could turn my head in any direction, so I was faced with the miserable prospect of a bumpy, two-hour journey to the medical centre in Sharjah. On seeing my distress, one of my soldiers took me to a quiet spot away from everyone else and told me to trust him and believe in his powers – about which until then I knew nothing at all. He started reading and quoting from the Koran, and occasionally blowing on my neck. As he blew, I realised that his breath was becoming hotter and hotter on my neck until it was similar to a burning sensation, and quite painful. Suddenly, he grabbed my head and twisted it; there was an audible click, and my head was back in place, with full movement miraculously restored. Mind over matter, call it what you like, but it worked. In my advancing years I frequently have to live with a painful neck on which no doctor or expensive treatment has had any effect, and I would dearly love to find that soldier again.

On many occasions I also witnessed that a few soldiers, on finding snakes or scorpions in the desert, would allow them to crawl or slide all over their bodies at will. Once the time came to release them, the other soldiers would have no hesitation in killing them, but only after the soldier who had handled them had looked away. It was explained to me that if the soldier saw them being killed he would lose his powers over them.

From time to time, Dhofari soldiers would request leave, stating they had just heard of a family death or sickness and needed to return home urgently. One must remember that this was long before the invention of all the communications gadgets we take for granted today. Nearly always, the soldier's story turned out to be true and I wondered how it was possible to learn such news from so far away so promptly. I was curious to find out, and was told it was possible to leave one's own body and travel to the home of a relative to see what was going on, as long as you only observed and did not try and make contact with them. My disbelief at this far-fetched explanation must have been obvious and one soldier who, according to the others, had this power offered to let me put it to the test. I was instructed to stand on his feet and concentrate on my parents at home in England. I went along with this and seriously thought about my parents all those thousands of miles away. Suddenly, I felt the most extraordinary sensation that I was somehow leaving my body and being transported elsewhere. This was all too much for me, and I let go of the soldier and put my feet firmly back into the sand; immediately everything was normal again. I have no idea whether, had I carried on with this mental test, I would have been able to see my parents or not, but I have a suspicion that I would have.

I also witnessed, on another occasion at a religious festival, worshippers of the Sufi faith dancing and chanting for hours and eventually going into what resembled a hypnotic trance. They then produced small knives, which they pushed into their bodies; not only did they not show any sign of pain but, on removing the knives, there was no entry wound or blood. I have no doubt it was genuine and once again it proved to me that there are many mysteries still out there for which we have no logical explanation. Others, including the Political Agent in Dubai, Donald Hawley, confirmed that he too had been present at a similar festival and observed the same ritual with the knives.

Occasionally, a Land Rover would appear from Sharjah, complete with a projector and sheet, to show a film, which was always very welcome and well attended. The soldiers had at one time been allowed to carry their rifles with them to watch films, but this was no longer the case because, on some occasions, especially if a western was being shown, the soldiers became rather excited and would shoot at the bad guys. Apart from destroying the 'screen,' arguments would continue well into the night about whether the cowboys or the Indians were the true villains. One night, the film being shown was the great epic, Lawrence of Arabia, and listening to the haunting music with sand dunes all around us added to the magic. At the end of the film, one of my young Arab officers asked me how old Lawrence was now. I did not understand the question and replied that Lawrence had died from injuries after a motorbike accident years ago, in the same way that we had just seen in the film. Shaking his head, the young officer said that he could not believe this was possible, as we had just been watching Lawrence and he was alive and well. My young officer was still confused, and reluctant to accept my explanation that we had only been watching a film on the life and times of Lawrence. I would have had an even greater problem to deal with if Peter O'Toole had suddenly decided to pay us a visit!

One problem we had in Support Group was that our ammunition allocation for training was limited, as it was very expensive, resulting in far too many 'dry' exercises. It was obviously important to keep up our skills but, without live firing, this could easily become rather monotonous. Fortunately, because we were the only unit to have the superior Dodge Power Wagons as our main means of transport, we spent a great deal of time patrolling and we were able to penetrate some of the more remote desert regions.

One area of great fascination to me was the vast remote expanse of sand and dunes that is aptly named the Empty Quarter, which must be one of the hottest places on Earth. It was very sparsely inhabited by nomadic tribesman who, with their families, camels and goats, somehow survived those harsh conditions. The first time I went there with some of my men was to take part in heat trials to evaluate how we performed in such hot conditions and to accurately measure our daily liquid intake and output. The medical team was led by an Australian doctor, who would have us drive or sometimes walk up incredibly steep sand dunes all day long, while he monitored our physical performance. During the trials we were allowed to drink as much water as we liked, provided we measured and recorded the amount that we drank; we also had a measuring glass for the 'output'. To the best of my recollection, I averaged a daily consumption of 32 pints, while I could only manage to squeeze out no more than half a pint of a very nasty dark liquid. The rest poured out of the body in sweat, similar to having a mobile shower.

In my early days, like most others, I would always carry a plentiful supply of salt tablets, essential to survive in the heat. It was only after taking part in heat trials that I learned that this was not the most effective method of absorbing salt into the body. The first test to complete was to find out if you actually needed salt, and a simple method would be to pour some salt onto a finger and lick it. If the body was really deficient in salt, it would taste sweet, rather like sugar. The best way to add salt to one's system is to sprinkle it in water rather than take a tablet, because the latter tends to remain concentrated on the lining of the stomach.

On another occasion we undertook a camel patrol into the really remote part of the Empty Quarter, hiring camels and the services of a trusted guide. Anyone who says that riding a camel is fun has either never ridden one or is basing their experience on a short trip around the Pyramids. Camels are uncomfortable and unpredictable, and they smell, fart and bite – and that's just in the first few minutes! Apart from that, these unfortunate camels can save your life, are capable of astonishing feats of endurance and are reasonably good to eat, especially when young. It would be fair to say, however, that I enjoy them more from a distance, rather like bagpipes and the harp.

The camel patrol we undertook was to be of two weeks' duration, self-sufficient in rations and with two radios in an attempt to keep in contact with Sharjah HQ. The aim of the patrol was, for some obscure reason, to visit and report on wells that had been identified and shown on a local map but never visited by the TOS. We would be totally reliant on our guide and his camels as none of us came from the area or had been in this extremely isolated part of the Empty Quarter before.

All went well for the first few days, basically camping at one well at night and then reaching another after a long, weary day in the saddle. How our guide navigated us through this vast expanse of desert with no landmarks, and the wind constantly changing the features and shape of the dunes, was beyond me.

We were completely at the mercy of our guide when not one but both our radios went on the blink. There we were, in the middle of nowhere, deprived of communication with the outside world. More than once, I questioned the wisdom of the patrol, and began to worry that I was not physically and mentally strong enough to endure the hardships we still had to face.

We arrived at one well for our evening camp but, on tasting the water, quickly found that it was far too brackish for human consumption. The camels did drink some, but even they were not impressed. It was our normal routine to fill up our water bags at each well we visited to ensure that we had sufficient for our needs until we reached the next one. On this occasion, we decided against replenishing our water supply because the water was so foul. This also eased the heavy load that our poor old 'ships of the desert' had to carry.

Because of this, we had to ration our limited water supply extremely carefully the next day, but we were not too concerned as our trusty guide assured us that the well we were heading for was not too far away, with the sweetest-tasting water ever. We rode on for hour after hour, with the guide advising, in response to frequent questions, that we were very close. This response was beginning to irritate both me and my soldiers, and doubts began to creep in about his navigational skills. All was forgiven when, there in the distance, we spotted the promised well and praises to Allah and the guide were gratefully given. However, our joy and happiness was short-lived when, on approaching the long-awaited watering hole, it became apparent that the well had collapsed and nothing remained but sand.

We were now in a very serious situation. We had no water, as we had put the well-being of the camels before our own, but at this stage even the bitter taste of the last brackish well-water would have been like nectar for us. It was obviously not the guide's fault that this well had caved in, but we now had to decide what our next move would be. The planned route we were taking was leading us further away from the scheduled RV, due in only a week's time. The question was whether to push on and hope the next well was in good working order or to retrace our steps to the well where at least we knew we could drink the water, brackish or not. By this time, our parched throats would have welcomed any liquid, irrespective of colour or taste. It made me remember my father's fine observation that there was no bad beer, but some tasted better than others!

I sat down with my soldiers and discussed the situation. We eventually decided that, rather than admit defeat, we would keep faith with our guide and press on regardless. We learned a serious lesson from this incident and realised that we should have filled up with the foul water rather than first consider the heavy load of the camel. We could then have poured it away once the next well was located and the water found to be acceptable. The day that followed was without doubt the longest that any of us had ever experienced, and that probably included the camels as well. Our previous sporadic outbursts of joking, singing or even conversation every day (normally about how far it would be to the next well) were replaced by silence and a grim determination to keep going and somehow hang in there to the eventual promised oasis. My tongue was stuck to the roof of my mouth and felt several inches thick. As the situation deteriorated, I made promises to myself that I would never take water, or any other liquid, for granted ever again if we survived the ordeal – which, as time went by, was not looking that certain.

I remember seeing a couple of aircraft passing miles above us, and in my mind I pictured those relaxed passengers enjoying a cold beer or gin and tonic with ice and lemon, looking down at the sea of sand beneath them and wondering if anything or anybody could survive down there. Late that afternoon, I detected a change in the guide's mood and even the camels seemed to perk up, especially when he pointed to a small object in the far distance. We all found some hidden reserve of energy from somewhere and managed certainly not a gallop, but a sort of trot, to reach the far-off well. To our indescribable relief and possible salvation, it was in working order, with the water tasting sweeter for me than any wine imaginable. It was only with great difficulty that we heeded the guide's instructions and only took frequent sips rather than an almighty downer.

Apart from one very tender part of my anatomy from spending so many days in the saddle, the rest of the patrol went fairly smoothly and we emerged alive and victorious, on time and at the right place. To be honest, I anticipated that we would receive a few compliments for our endurance and the hardships we had suffered, but I only received a bollocking for losing radio contact. Life can be very cruel, especially in the Empty Quarter. I am certain that the few of us who took part in that unique patrol will never forget it and it is my hope that, with the help of the campfire and coffee pot, the story of that adventure will continue to be told.

It also brought home to me how vulnerable and precarious life can be, and the simple pleasures that I had taken for granted before my experience on that camel patrol suddenly became very special and appreciated.

On our return to our base camp at Manama, we settled in to our more conventional military lifestyle and training once again. Not only were we proud of our efficiency and high standards with our mortars and machine guns in Support Group, but we were a formidable force with the rifle as well. Every year, a rifle meeting was held at Manama, hotly contested by all the squadrons, including support units and invited teams from the various police forces. In 1967 we were delighted to win our way through to the final, once again proving our proud boast that, although we were only a small unit, we could take on and beat the best. In the final, we came across a team from Dubai with HH Sheikh Mohammed bin Rashid Al Maktoum, a young son of the Ruler, not only in charge, but already well known as a determined and fierce competitor. It was a falling plate event, with each team firing initially from 300 metres, then running through the sand and finishing at 200 metres, with the first team to knock down all their plates the winners. As team leaders, both Sheikh Mohammed and I sized each other's teams up and I noticed that, because his team members were in civilian dress, they had removed their sandals. This gave them a speed advantage over our military footwear, which was heavy and would slow us down considerably. My objection to their being able to compete barefooted was overruled, much to the delight of Sheikh Mohammed, who probably thought that my challenge was not the correct sporting action of 'an officer and a gentleman'. Sure enough, we could not match their speed through the sand and our team finished a much slower second. In fairness, I believed they were the better team, and only found out later that they had been discreetly practising for a long time in preparation for this event. It is common knowledge today that Sheikh Mohammed, now the Ruler of Dubai, takes everything he is involved in very seriously and is highly motivated, especially in the sporting arena. I was privileged to experience his fine qualities at first hand all those years ago and it comes as no surprise to me that Dubai has prospered so incredibly well under his rule.

Life in Support Group was certainly never boring. We were frequently sent on vehicle patrols and the occasional donkey patrol, which I thoroughly enjoyed. It was therefore quite a shock when I was called in to Sharjah HQ and informed that Support Group had been selected for ceremonial guard duties. Marching up and down on a parade square had never featured as part of our regular training programme.

I had been informed that the Ruler of Kuwait, HH Sheikh Sabah Al Salim Al Sabah, was scheduled to visit the Trucial States and, as the rulers of Ajman, Sharjah and Ras Al Khaimah had no troops of their own, they had requested that the Scouts provide a Guard of Honour in each State. This startling discovery meant that we suddenly had to practise and remember drill formations and words of command we all thought were history, and to make sure our uniforms and appearance were of the highest order. Our first parade was in Sharjah, where a huge excited crowd assembled to greet the Emir from the already wealthy oil state. Expectations were also understandably running high that all the states would benefit from his generosity. Every drill movement we carried out was greeted with an appreciative roar and applause which, apart from being unexpected, made it very difficult to make my spoken orders heard. The Ruler of Kuwait, accompanied by the recently installed Ruler of Sharjah, HH Sheikh Khalid bin Muhammed Al Qasimi, emerged onto the saluting dais to even more thunderous applause. Probably the loudest appreciation from the crowd came when they witnessed a British officer from the TOS approach, salute the rulers with his sword, and then address them in Arabic. That brought the house down!

We repeated this Guard of Honour twice more, conducting the last in Ras Al Khaimah. By now the Emir was beginning to recognise me and greet me like an old friend. I was even more pleasantly surprised when, after our last ceremonial duty, I was told that he wanted to meet me in the reception room where the local dignitaries were gathered. I waited for my turn to be introduced and was rather taken back when he invited me to sit with him. We exchanged pleasantries in Arabic, which seemed to impress him, but, as I went to take my leave, he told me to sit and wait for a moment. The Emir summoned one of his aides, and thoughts of a possible gold watch flashed through my mind, only to be dashed when a photographer suddenly appeared in front of us. He proceeded to take a photo of the Emir and me sitting together and I was assured by the Emir that I would receive a copy in due course as a souvenir of the visit. I did eventually receive an old brown envelope addressed to me. Inside the envelope was a postcard-sized photograph, resembling a London fog, with two seated shadowy figures, totally unrecognisable, apart from their sets of smiling teeth.

Although my Support Group and I participated in various formal historical events, these could not begin to compare with a historic political event in which we took part soon after my return in 1966. During the five years I had been away from the Gulf, many changes had been taking place due to the discovery of oil. Both Abu Dhabi and Dubai had begun to receive enormous incomes generated from their oil production and contract concessions, but it was more in Dubai than Abu Dhabi that these changes first became visible.

There were many rumours surrounding the supposed inability of Sheikh Shakhbut, the Ruler of Abu Dhabi, to comprehend the potential of this vast income, and it was whispered that he insisted in being paid in new currency notes. Further allegations emerged that huge amounts of cash were stored in his mud-walled palace, even under his bed, and that weevils and rodents had devoured a great deal of this fortune. It was also reputed that, when he was persuaded to use the local branch of the British Bank of the Middle East to hold the cash, he would make impromptu visits to the bank and demand to see all his wealth, which meant hurriedly flying-in charter aircraft to deliver the goods.

On a more serious note, it was obvious that Sheikh Shakhbut was having severe difficulties coming to terms with this sudden transition. He was a good traditional tribal ruler, but he now had the added responsibility of overseeing the management and practical administration necessary to transform his state, which had quickly become one of the wealthiest in the world in per capita terms.

Unbeknown to lowly mortals such as me, high-powered talks had been taking place discreetly for a considerable time between the British government and some members of the ruling family on how to resolve the situation.

The history of the Abu Dhabi rulers is a complex one, littered with coups. Sheikh Shakhbut had been in power as ruler since 1928. This in itself was quite a remarkable achievement, as none of the four previous rulers had lasted for more than a few years, and only one of them had died peacefully. There was growing frustration within the ruling family at the lack of modernisation and progress that should have resulted from the oil revenue. There were also serious concerns that Sheikh Shakhbut's frugal policy could undermine the stability of Abu Dhabi and lead to civil unrest.

The other, less fortunate, states to the north of Abu Dhabi were also displeased that their wealthy neighbour continued to be reluctant to make any significant contribution towards the TSDF, which would be of immense benefit to all.

Thanks to certain official documents now available to the public, it is possible to reconstruct the initial discussions that had been held over a three-year period. Sheikh Zayed, in particular, had held informal discussions with close family members in an effort to formulate an acceptable peaceful plan to replace Sheikh Shakhbut and make Zayed ruler. Another delicate family issue that also required careful consideration was the promise that both Shakhbut and Zayed had given to their mother. She had made them swear an oath to her that there would never be blood spilt between them. Their concerned mother was obviously well aware of the past violent family history and understandably hoped that this maternal intervention would guarantee that there would be no recurrence of family feuding. One probable reason for the reluctance of Sheikh Shakhbut to open up the overflowing coffers or to spend much of his vast available wealth, was that he realised this would mean he would lose considerable personal control in his territories. In the past, such a loss would have been seen as a sign of weakness, with predictable consequences.

Increasingly, Sheikh Zayed became the focus of attention, and it is well documented that, in discussions with members of the British government, he had made known his views about his brother. His main concerns were about the latter's lack of commitment to modernisation, and on numerous occasions he had even expressed doubts about Sheikh Shakhbut's sanity. Sheikh Zayed also believed strongly that Abu Dhabi's wealth should be shared by all the states, not retained by Abu Dhabi alone. He had deservedly earned the reputation in Al Ain of being a truly great, caring leader, with concern for the welfare of all in the Trucial States.

It is apparent from correspondence now available to the general public that a plan to depose Sheikh Shakhbut was in place in 1963, but was not carried out. At the last moment, some family members hesitated and withdrew their support for Sheikh Zayed. Once again, it was a case of 'back to the drawing board' to come up with a solution that required the approval of the entire close ruling family. There had been considerable propaganda from Arab nationalists about the British involvement in the recent removal of Sheikh Saqr of Sharjah, and any obvious show of British force to replace the all-important ruler of an oil-rich sheikhdom would have had far-reaching repercussions throughout the entire Arab world. It was correctly presumed that the other six Trucial State rulers would welcome the appointment of Sheikh Zayed as the Abu Dhabi ruler. They were well aware of his commitment to the improvement of all the states and were frustrated at the lack of financial support they were receiving from his brother. It was now all down to the ruling family to come to terms with the idea and to give their blessing and support to Sheikh Zayed. Although most of them fully supported Sheikh Zayed and realised the need for a change in leadership, it remained a major obstacle for them to support Sheikh Zayed openly. Sheikh Shakhbut was still a strong tribal leader and, with good cause, they feared the repercussions that would be inflicted on them should he hear of their plans to remove him.

Numerous proposals had been discussed on how best to replace Shakhbut with his brother, including the possibility of staging a coup when Shakhbut was out of the country. One suggestion even contemplated his removal while he was sailing on the expensive yacht he had purchased from Prince Rainier of Monaco!

The relevant official UK documents covering the period leading up to the removal of Sheikh Shakhbut in August 1966 still remain classified, despite the normal 30-year closure period having long since expired. It can therefore only be presumed that Sheikh Zayed managed to procure the written consent of all the powerful members of the ruling family to support the removal of Sheikh Shakhbut. The letter would then have been delivered to Mr Nuttall, the acting Political Agent in Dubai. Once this final piece of the plan was received, hasty discussions took place on the possible requirement for the TOS to provide military backup, and an operational strategy was put into action.

One Scouts officer, Jon Cousins, an intelligence officer, who was very close to Sheikh Zayed, most certainly did know what was happening. He was actively involved as the various stages of the plan developed but, as a professional soldier, never gave anything away at the time. His role in events was that of messenger, carrying highly confidential correspondence between the main participants planning the replacement of Sheikh Shakhbut. Jon recalls that, when he handed Sheikh Zayed the letter from the Political Agent to confirm the family decision and the use of the TOS, he had to point out to Sheikh Zayed that he needed to sign the letter. Sheikh Zayed gave Jon a big smile and then complied. As an intelligence officer, Jon was also well aware that, apart from the concerns of the ruling family, there was considerable unrest within the Buraimi Oasis and as far away as the Liwa, 100 km inland. This volatile situation had the potential to lead to mass demonstrations to confront Sheikh Shakhbut 'head on' unless there was an acceptable solution. Jon deserves great credit for the vital role he played as a go-between, which finally enabled Sheikh Zayed to become the ruler of Abu Dhabi.

(It was known that Jon had a passion for flying and in 1967 he flew a light aircraft from England to Sharjah, and then continued on to Abu Dhabi and Al Ain. One day, shortly after Sheikh Zayed had become Ruler, a friend of Jon's who worked as a confidential secretary to the Sheikh informed Jon that Abu Dhabi needed its own airline, and enquired if he would like to set it up. Jon jumped at the proposal and a few days later received a formal letter signed by Sheikh Zayed authorising him to set up a limited company in Abu Dhabi to become its national airline. It was explained that, until there was a company law, such a letter – a decree, in effect – was the only means of setting up a limited company. Jon was also advised that this gesture by Sheikh Zayed was in recognition of his 'services rendered'. Sadly, the project never materialised because Jon presumed that Sheikh Zayed's vision for a union of all the States would also require one single airline operated by all the Gulf States. This would mean the establishment of a much larger airline, able to compete with major European and US flag carriers. Jon modestly felt he was not qualified to establish and control such an organisation, and declined. He did pursue a career in aviation, however, and on leaving the army joined Gulf Aviation.)

Back in Manama, hot as hell and with my feet firmly on the ground, on 5 August I received instructions that we were to move with our machine-gun sections from Manama to the Abu Dhabi crossroads, fully equipped for any eventuality. We were to be in position by first light the next morning, when we would be fully briefed. It was obvious that something of significance was about to happen, as the radio link to various outstations was working overtime. It was no easy task for us to load up and travel by night to ensure arrival at the old coffee shop at the crossroads on the outskirts of Abu Dhabi exactly at the appointed hour. Somehow we managed it, and of course all conversation between us had been dominated by our curiosity over the sudden urgency of the move and the possible reasons behind it.

We did not have to wait long to be briefed, and were informed that a decision had been taken by the Abu Dhabi ruling family to depose Sheikh Shakhbut and replace him with his brother. It was hoped that this would be achieved in a courteous, peaceful manner, and would not require military action. Our role in this plan was to stop all civilian traffic into Abu Dhabi and to act as backup in case the transfer of power did not go smoothly. Armed resistance from the Abu Dhabi Defence Force, which had been set up by Sheikh Shakhbut, was not anticipated, and it was considered highly unlikely that we would be called on to advance on Abu Dhabi with machine guns blazing! 'A' Squadron TOS was to be located close to the palace where Sheikh Shakhbut was in residence, in case military intervention were required.

On the morning of 6 August 1966, Glen Balfour Paul, who, along with Sir William Luce, had been instrumental in all the negotiations leading up to this historic day, paid a call on Sheikh Shakhbut. He informed him of the ruling family's decision to replace him. By all accounts, this news was met with angry defiance, but he was eventually persuaded that his rule was over and any attempt to resist would result in the use of the TOS to enforce the decision. The Abu Dhabi Defence Force, commanded by ex-TOS officer Tug Wilson, had earlier been ordered to return to barracks and had complied. Finally, after several hours of heated negotiations, Sheikh Shakhbut was escorted out of his palace with his family by my old friend Lt Obaid Ali from X Squadron. They left the palace peacefully, in a dignified manner, much to the relief of those present or who had been involved in this delicate operation. As Sheikh Shakhbut left his palace, a Guard of Honour was mounted out of respect for him. This had been organised at short notice by Mike Curtis of A Squadron, which had been closely involved in the operation (as described in his book, *Arabian Days*). Sheikh Zayed also directed that the removal of his brother as ruler was not to be celebrated as it was a sad day, and that people must respect these wishes.

This was a necessary but emotional step forward, which enabled Abu Dhabi to take its rightful position in the world under the wise and visionary rule of Sheikh Zayed and brought prosperity and unity to more than just Abu Dhabi. For my part, I am proud that my Support Group was there on that historic day, even though we were only deployed on the outskirts of Abu Dhabi and in a backup role.

My first 18 months with the Scouts were coming to an end and I successfully applied for a second tour; I was looking forward to the future with my Support Group. I think the King's Regiment had written me off as a lost cause to the desert. They had correctly pointed out that it was not in my interest as a professional soldier to overstay my service in Arabia and that I should return to a more conventional military life. One of the main criticisms I frequently heard from our Arab officers was that very few of us ever served long enough in the TOS to come to terms with and understand the customs, history and traditions of the Gulf and to become fluent in Arabic. These were very valid points and I was interested to read recently that in June 1961 Sheikh Zayed himself, while still the Governor of Al Ain, complained to the then Political Agent, Donald Hawley, that more British officers like Ian Craig-Adams were needed to ensure effective continuity. I recall visiting a squadron commander who happened to be dealing with a disciplinary case involving one of his soldiers. I waited outside the tent where the proceedings were taking place and could not help but overhear the major telling the confused soldier in Arabic that he was always a good soldier and never a bad one. I thought that this was rather strange as the soldier was on a disciplinary charge, but he thanked his squadron commander for the compliment, which made the major more and more irate. Discreetly, I popped my head in, and told my colleague he had the Arabic for always and never the wrong way round! Our soldiers quickly understood our less-than-perfect Arabic, but the Bedouin we came into contact with were generally at a loss to make any sense of our strange accents. Many of the Bedouin, especially in the more remote areas, were not used to meeting white men and had difficulty in accepting that these pale or red-skinned strangers could actually speak their language.

Not long into my second tour, I was called to HQ in Sharjah to see Colonel Pat Ive, the new Commander, TOS. He was a delightful, happy man, and soon deservedly won the respect of all of us.

I could hardly believe the Colonel's words when he informed me there had been some internal problems with B Squadron and the decision had been taken to hand the command over to me, with promotion to major. I was still only 29 years old at the time so, despite the well-intentioned warning from my regiment, things were turning out pretty well, in terms of both rank and salary.

'SHINY B'

Naturally, it was hard to come to terms with leaving the men of dear old 'Three Inch', with whom I had shared so many fantastic experiences. But I was comforted by the challenge of returning to 'Shiny B', which, by all accounts, was a bit low on morale. The Squadron was once again stationed in Jahili Fort at Al Ain, where I had first met up with Ian Craig-Adams and, although he was no longer around, I could feel his presence everywhere. Quite a few of the soldiers from my first tour were still with the squadron, so it was more of a homecoming, which made my job much easier and greatly helped me in gaining their confidence and trust.

I also had Rashid Abdulla Al Shamsi, one of the most amazing men that I have been fortunate to serve with, as my Sergeant Major. He looked the part, and was a strict disciplinarian on parade, but also a caring human being to whom I could always turn for sensible advice.

In no time at all, 'Shiny B' was back to its former glory days and we all made the most of the short time we had left at Jahili. I also thoroughly enjoyed having the room at the top of the tower for the first time, with its panoramic views of the surrounding desert and, more importantly, a cool breeze.

Being stationed at Al Ain also gave me the opportunity and privilege to get to know HH Sheikh Khalifa bin Zayed Al Nahyan, who had taken over from his father as the Ruler's Representative in Al Ain. Sheikh Khalifa took a keen interest in our squadron and its activities in Al Ain and I met him on a regular basis to discuss matters of mutual interest. At one such meeting, shortly before our departure from Al Ain, Sheikh Khalifa requested that my squadron should march through the town in a farewell parade. This was a great compliment as, to the best of my knowledge, it was the first time any resident squadron in Al Ain had been given this honour. We duly marched through the town, with our splendid Regimental Pipes and Drums Band leading the way. The whole town seemed to turn out to cheer us on enthusiastically and His Highness acknowledged our salute as we marched past him. It was a very special day for all of us in 'Shiny B', and I know we all felt immensely proud and appreciated the applause and support the people of Al Ain gave us. To hear bagpipes being played in the middle of the desert was also quite special, and to this day bagpipes can still be heard in military and police bands in the Gulf. The parade was followed by a magnificent banquet of camel and goat meat generously provided by Sheikh Khalifa, and vast quantities were consumed by all of us.

I have always enjoyed the Arab *fuddle*, with huge amounts of meat and rice served on large trays and strictly eaten with only the right hand. It did not take long, while sitting on the ground or carpet, to become proficient at forming a ball of rice and meat and popping it into one's mouth, but I did have a problem with the contents of the goat's head. It was customary for the host to expertly break open the head and offer parts of the brains, tongue and eye to his honoured guests, as these morsels are considered to be delicacies. It would not only be considered impolite to decline these tasty offerings, but also not understood, as only a few prominent guests would be lucky enough to receive them, much to the envy of the others. I became quite crafty at pushing pieces of brain and tongue deep into the rice for some surprised 'second sitting' diner to discover with great glee. To dispose of the eye was not as easy, as it would normally be placed into your hand with little or no chance for concealment. I am also certain that most of my Arab friends were fully aware that most of we Westerners did not share their taste for an eye, and much amusement was discreetly had watching us trying to swallow one without choking on it.

In those days life was more relaxed and it was possible to call on a ruler or anyone else in high authority relatively easily, and I have happy memories of time spent with many of these great leaders. I remember vividly our new CO, Colonel Pat Ive, visiting us at Fort Jahili and an audience being arranged with Sheikh Zayed, who was in the area at the time. The three of us sat on the ground in the desert with a retinue, as always, of tribesman armed with a variety of weapons (including old muzzle-loaders) close at hand. Colonel Pat briefed Sheikh Zayed on important relevant military matters, and then Sheikh Zayed brought us up to date with some of the new and exciting plans he had for the region. He mentioned that a road would be built into the Liwa close to the Empty Quarter, which would open it up and make this remote area more accessible. I must have looked concerned at this news, as Sheikh Zayed, who by now I knew extremely well, asked me what was troubling me. I replied that in the past I had enjoyed the challenge and excitement I had experienced having to travel by camel or vehicle over the vast sand dunes to reach this isolated desert location and I would miss that. Sheikh Zayed looked me firmly in the eye and, with his wonderful smile, which was nearly always present, told me that my problem was I wanted to be more Bedouin than the Bedouin themselves! He went on that if I would miss travelling over the desert dunes in the future, I could always drive off the tarmac road and proceed as in the past. Who could argue with that?

King Hussein of Jordan was another great leader I was privileged to meet in Al Ain. The King was on an official visit to the Trucial States and Al Ain was included in his itinerary. His more moderate approach with Israel did little to enhance his popularity with the people of the area, and he was not as well received as he had been in the past. Some donkeys, with his portrait on them, were even galloped along the route that he would take, which was a huge insult. In my opinion, this courageous and far-sighted monarch did not deserve this disgraceful treatment, but it was not possible for me to intervene in an internal, peaceful demonstration.

I attended the lunch given in the King's honour, but it was obvious from the poor attendance that many of the local dignitaries had boycotted the event. From time to time I could see the King looking in my direction, probably wondering who this Englishman was, dressed up in Arab headdress. When the lunch was over, there was a delay while transport was being called, which meant that for a short time the King was seated there on his own, but he didn't show any sign of annoyance or embarrassment.

On impulse I went over to him, saluted, and introduced myself, and was pleasantly surprised when His Majesty asked me to sit with him. It was apparent from our conversation that he had a good knowledge of the TOS and its role in the Gulf and also knew that we had started sending some of our young Arab officers to Jordan for training. He asked me if any of our British seconded officers had visited our officers in training in Jordan, and I had to reply that I was not aware of any such visit. King Hussein then pointedly informed me that this should be rectified and that I should convey this message to my CO.

This was duly done, and there is no prize for guessing who was sent to Jordan to spend a few days with our young Arab officers undergoing training there. They much appreciated the visit, and I also thoroughly enjoyed the opportunity to see a little of a country I had always wanted to visit. I was impressed by the military standards and traditions that I observed and it helped me understand why the Jordanian army was so well regarded by other forces. Unfortunately, during my time in Jordan the King was away, but I was assured by one of his military aides that he would be informed of my visit. The aide also promised to make sure His Majesty was made aware that the officer who had visited was the one who he had met briefly in Al Ain.

It is a strange and small world, and some while later my niece Frances went to work in Jordan as the personal assistant to the King's wife, Queen Noor. Frances was able to recount to King Hussein our meeting at Al Ain and she told me that His Majesty remembered it well and regretted not being in Jordan at the time of my visit, as he would have been interested to meet me again. I strongly believe that King Hussein was a truly brave, visionary Arab leader who deserves far greater recognition for his tireless efforts in attempting, against massive obstacles, to achieve the dream of a peaceful Middle East.

The rifle squadrons were relocated every six to eight months in an exercise named Operation Roundabout. This was a sensible policy that ensured that we did not get too close to the local people, which could jeopardise our neutrality, and also took into account that some locations were harder to live in than others. The remote, humid Mirfa was a classic example of this, while Masafi in the mountains and Fort Jahili in Al Ain were considered the best outstations.

Around the middle of 1968, while we were still stationed at Fort Jahili, but with Operation Roundabout not far off, I was called to the HQ in Sharjah for an important briefing to be given by Colonel Pat Ive and Major Tim Budd. Tim had served in the TOS since 1955 and was another of the truly great characters. Because of his long service, he had acquired an immense knowledge of the people and the tribes. Once again, this clearly showed the value of continuity and, as a result, Tim was the ideal Force Intelligence Officer, well qualified to pass on his wealth of experience to all new officers joining the TOS. During this briefing, I was informed that HH Sheikh Saqr bin Mohammed Al Qasimi, the Ruler of Ras

Al Khaimah, had, for the first time in the history of the TOS, given his permission for a rifle squadron to be based in Ras Al Khaimah's territory. The campsite was to be on a gravel plain towards the Agricultural Research Farm at Dig Dagga on the outskirts of Ras Al Khaimah, and had the memorable name of Hum Hum. This was an important breakthrough as our political masters were of the opinion that Sheikh Saqr would not be fully supportive of the proposed merger and formation of the United Arab Emirates when Britain withdrew its protective role at the end of 1971. They thought that Sheikh Saqr was less cooperative than some of the other rulers and more independently minded. With this in mind, the importance and significance of a squadron being located in Ras Al Khaimah was repeatedly stressed to me. Then, much to my delight and surprise, I was told that my squadron, 'Shiny B', had been given the honour of being the first squadron to be based at this new camp. It was also pointed out that it was essential for me personally to get off to a good start with the ruler and to make sure we did nothing to make him regret his decision to allow a TOS camp in Ras Al Khaimah. In addition, the hope was expressed by the Foreign Office that allowing a TOS presence in Ras Al Khaimah might influence Sheikh Saqr to adopt a more conciliatory approach to the proposed United Arab Emirates.

Mixing politics with soldiering has usually been a recipe for disaster, but we were entering delicate, uncharted waters with no past history to turn to for guidance. 'Shiny B' was rightly proud to be chosen as the first TOS permanent unit in Ras Al Khaimah, and we moved into our new camp not really sure what to expect.

Our mainly tented camp, about half an hour out of Ras Al Khaimah, was quite isolated, with camels and goats grazing nearby on the thorny bushes that thrived on the gravel plain. We also had the stunning Hajar mountain range as a backdrop in the distance. Nigel Harris was my very capable and reliable second-in-command (2i/c), and his loyal support made my command much less of a daunting challenge. He also turned out to be an excellent master builder, supervising the construction of a fireplace and a small swimming pool (from materials obtained from questionable sources), which considerably improved our personal lives in the Officers' Mess. I have made a point of visiting the camp site at Hum Hum on return visits and, although most of the old buildings have been rather neglected, the hut that served as our Officers' Mess survives and the fireplace and swimming pool are still there, not only as remnants of the colonial past, but as a tribute to Nigel's building ability!

On my initial deployment to the Hum Hum camp, one of my first duties was to pay a courtesy call on Sheikh Saqr to thank him for permitting the camp to be established in his territory. His modest home and offices were adjacent to each other and his son, Sheikh Khalid, the Crown Prince, lived opposite. I had met the ruler on several previous occasions but I had never had a private audience with him, so I was very much on my best behaviour. I was also more than a little apprehensive about the meeting, especially after my briefing about the importance of our being stationed in Ras Al Khaimah territory. At this first meeting, the Crown Prince and the Ruler's Lebanese financial advisor, Tawfiq Abu Khatr, were also in attendance but the Ruler was quite clearly in charge. Sheikh Saqr bin Mohammed Al Qasimi was of medium height, quietly spoken, and with no apparent distinguishing features other than a glass eye, which was thought to be the result of an incident as a youth. Unless forewarned, as I had been, the glass eye was not really noticeable and never mentioned. (Among the countless theories put forward, some suggested it was the result of a hawk pecking him on a hunting trip, and even a chicken had been mentioned. HH Sheikh Saud recently told me the truth about how his father had lost his eye. The reality was that, as a boy, Sheikh Saqr had fallen off his camel and his eye had been so badly damaged that it had been removed.)

The Ruler's office was by no means lavishly furnished, apart from a tall stand bearing an ornate telephone, which rang frequently and was answered each time by His Highness in person. Sheikh Saqr had a pleasant, easy manner and appeared genuinely interested in hearing how my squadron would be of assistance to his state. As our discussion continued, it was clear that we each understood the significance of the TOS being based in Ras Al Khaimah for the first time, and the responsibilities that would fall on us. Following the traditional Arabic coffee and polite initial conversation, Sheikh Saqr then welcomed my squadron to Ras Al Khaimah and briefed me on the strained relationship that existed with some of the mountain tribes. He continued that he hoped our presence would assist with restoring a more peaceful environment for the good of all, and expressed the wish that this would be the start of a long association with the TOS. He assured me of his full support and that I could call on him or the Crown Prince at any time. He also accepted my invitation to visit the new Hum Hum camp in the near future. The meeting went very well and after I bade farewell to the Ruler, the Crown Prince, who spoke fluent English, escorted me to my vehicle, making me feel very much at ease. I left feeling well satisfied that this all-important first meeting had achieved far more than I had initially expected.

The squadron soon established a good routine, concentrating on frequent patrols in an attempt to improve the relationship between us and the tribesmen. To achieve this important dialogue I was given huge assistance by Tim Ash, the local TOS Intelligence Officer, who had deservedly gained the respect and trust of everyone in the territory over the years. The main cause for concern came from two mountain tribes, the Shehhu and the Hebus, who traditionally carried a small axe for protection but now also carried a variety of firearms. These tribesmen and their families lived high up in the Hajar Mountains in remote stone houses that were accessible only on foot or by donkey. One of the persistent causes of dispute was the vaguely defined borders, especially in the mountainous region to the east of Ras Al Khaimah towards the Batinah coast. There had been long-standing feudal disputes in these areas, where the various tribes laid claim to certain territories. These claims were difficult to settle as some regions belonged to Oman and some to Ras Al Khaimah, while some were claimed by Sharjah. Historically there had always been problems between the Shehhu, the Hebus and the Qawasim rulers of Ras Al Khaimah. Frequently during the summer months many of the mountain tribesmen would move their families to the coastal area of Ras Al Khaimah, in particular Sharm. While living on the coast, they would accept that they owed their allegiance to the Ruler of Ras Al Khaimah but, when it suited them, they would change to become loyal subjects of the far distant Sultan of Oman!

At the small port of Khor Khowair, in the north of Ras Al Khaimah, a German company had been granted mining rights for the high-quality stone that could be extracted from the mountains. To facilitate this, the company established a quarry in the area and built a jetty to transport the stone by sea. The Shehhu took offence at this activity as they considered that the company was 'eating their mountain' with their large machines, and they made their displeasure known by frequently firing into the quarry company's camp with their old muzzle-loaders. After such incidents there would be local negotiations that would normally resolve the situation, but it was an ongoing problem that had to be dealt with on a regular basis.

Being fully aware of this constant local unrest, I expected that these mischievous mountain men would cause many of the major problems that arose during our time in Ras Al Khaimah. It was therefore a complete surprise when I was briefed by Tim Ash about a possible tribal revolt against the Ruler that was being planned, not by the Shehhu or the Hebus, but by another prominent leader by the name of Saif bin Ali. He was the chief of the influential Khawater tribe and it was well known that he was critical of and outspoken over what he considered to be the slow pace of development in Ras Al Khaimah, compared to the progress now being achieved in the oil-rich states of Abu Dhabi and Dubai. His critical outbursts were all the more surprising as Sheikh Saqr was married to one of Saif bin Ali's sisters.

Tim Ash's intelligence reports were well founded. in late 1968, Saif bin Ali had called on local tribesmen to rebel against Sheikh Saqr and it was soon discovered that he had assembled well over 100 loyal armed tribesmen to support his cause. These included representatives from the mountain tribes and they had gathered on a relatively high hill near Hamraniya, not far from our camp. On learning of this, Sheikh Saqr immediately requested assistance from the Political Agent in Dubai to put down the armed rebellion and once this request had been approved the matter was passed on to the TOS to resolve. My squadron, being located in the right place at the right time, received instructions that I was to deal with the situation and to restore order with the minimum of force and casualties to both sides. I requested dear old Support Group, which was still based nearby at Manama, to be called up to assist us. They arrived promptly under the command of my very capable replacement, Miles Stockwell, who was clearly relishing the prospect of putting their skills to the test.

Sergeant Major Rashid and I discussed the merits of various options open to us if force was needed to achieve our aim. The main problem was that, as the tribesmen occupied the easily defended high ground, any assault would result in a serious loss of life on both sides. It would have been a relatively simple exercise to surround the feature and call on Saif bin Ali to lay down his arms or face an assault on his position. He would more than likely refuse, and then be subjected to mortar fire before a final assault on his position. This action would certainly result in heavy casualties among the rebels, but would make it a relatively easy and safe task for me to then move in with my troops and arrest the ringleaders without much resistance. This would have been rather like using a heavy fist to swat a fly, and would have been effective, but was hardly likely to win the approval of other tribes in the region or the Political Agent.

After lengthy deliberations I eventually made my decision and, to Sergeant Major Rashid's disbelief, informed him of my simple plan of action. The two of us would drive in our Land Rover as far as possible up the hill towards the assembled well-armed tribesmen and would then continue, unarmed, on foot to the top. There we would arrest Saif bin Ali and then escort him back to Ras Al Khaimah, and hand him over to the Ruler. A strategically well thought-out and straightforward, simple plan! I am not sure if Rashid had ever heard about mad dogs and Englishman going out in the midday sun but, from the look he gave me, he obviously thought that I had flipped. I explained that he would use a loudhailer to inform Saif of our intentions and ensure he clearly understood that if we were shot on our ascent to meet him, or if any harm came to us while holding talks with him, both he and his rebels would be subjected to the full might of the assembled TOS forces. The highly competent and likeable Ian Stewart had replaced Nigel Harris as my Squadron 2i/c but, for some reason, he was not present during this operational decision-making. The fact that he was not aware of my plan was probably a good thing, as he may well have come to the same conclusion as Rashid, that the sun had taken its toll on me, and requested my immediate medical evacuation.

With my squadron and Support Group in position, Rashid called to Saif bin Ali and told him repeatedly with the loudhailer that just the two of us were going to make our way up to meet him and negotiate an end to the situation. We drove up the hill as far as we could and then proceeded on foot, trying to demonstrate clearly that we were unarmed. I recall that I kept telling Rashid to keep reminding the rebels through his loudhailer that we had no weapons and that there would be serious consequences if we were shot. The only response we received from the tribesmen looking down at us as we slowly made our way up to meet them was rifle fire. A steady stream of bullets greeted us on our gradual ascent, hitting the sand on both sides of us and close enough for us to feel the impact. Not surprisingly, we felt incredibly vulnerable, but we also hoped that this rebel strategy was deliberate, as it was clear that if they had wanted to shoot us their aim would have been spot-on. At least, that was what the two of us said to each other for reassurance, but I don't think either of us was too convinced. We certainly felt completely at the rebels' mercy when we finally approached the summit with bullets landing ever closer to us. On finally reaching the rebel position and in an attempt to appear to be in control of the situation, I demanded that Saif show himself.

He did appear, and Rashid and I felt as if we had entered the 'lion's den' as we realised that we were now surrounded by a reception committee of well over 100 very angry, well-armed tribesmen who were obviously not overly amused by our

presence. In fact they were downright hostile! We then sat with Saif and some
of his senior supporters, and over coffee we made polite conversation inquiring
about each other's health and that of our families. This was most bizarre as only
moments before they had been shooting at us, but that appeared to be forgotten
and traditional praise was given to Allah that we were all safe and well. I did
wonder, given the hostile looks on their faces, how much longer our good health
would last.

After several hours of negotiations, Saif was eventually persuaded to come
round to our way of thinking, that it was not in anyone's interest to prolong his
dispute with the Ruler. In particular, we eventually made him realise the futility of
the situation and the inevitable loss of life and casualties that would be suffered by
both sides if he continued to escalate the rebellion. Sergeant Major Rashid, who
was naturally our spokesman, did an excellent, eloquent job of convincing Saif
bin Ali to accept the reality of the situation, while I nodded my head vigorously
in agreement with Rashid. I also made a great show of pointing out to Saif bin Ali
the proximity of our troops and mortars waiting to assault his position, should it
be necessary. In the negotiations to end this 'revolt', Saif bin Ali's main concern
was understandably about what would be his punishment if he gave the order
for his followers to lay down their weapons peacefully and decided to surrender.
With justification, he expressed his concern that Sheikh Saqr would wish to
make an example of him to deter others from similar acts of defiance. Saif bin Ali
genuinely feared for his life.

On the spur of the moment and with no vested authority, I gave Saif my word
that I would only hand him over to the Ruler once Sheikh Saqr had personally
given me his promise that Saif would not come to any physical harm. On
the strength of that commitment and with a quizzical concerned look in my
direction from Sergeant Major Rashid, Saif bin Ali and his cousin Obaid agreed
to surrender, but made it very clear that they were trusting me to honour the
assurance I had given them.

The tribesmen, who were surrounding us and listening attentively to every
word, allowed us to leave with their leaders but they made it very clear that we
would not have a very healthy future or a long life if the two of us did not keep our
word. We reached the Land Rover and, with an escort quickly assembled from my
squadron, departed for Ras Al Khaimah with an apprehensive Saif and his cousin
sitting quietly by my side. I could not help asking myself if these two tribal leaders

were wondering whether they had done the right thing and how much they could rely on the word of an Englishman. As we approached the Ruler's residence, I told the escort in charge of Saif and Obaid to wait until I had had the opportunity to meet with Sheikh Saqr. Only then would I be in a position to gauge his reaction and learn his decision about my promise of safety to his subjects who had openly rebelled against him.

The Ruler was delighted to receive my news that all had been resolved peacefully, but more than a little surprised to hear that Saif and his cousin were outside and had handed themselves over without any resistance. I had to explain to His Highness that I had given my word that they would not receive physical punishment, and respectfully informed him that, if he did not accept this condition, I would have no alternative but to take my prisoners to the TOS HQ in Sharjah, where they would be detained while waiting for a decision from the Political Agent. Sheikh Saqr listened attentively, thought for a moment, and then said he was happy that there had been no loss of life and agreed that Saif and Obaid should spend some time in prison and would then be released unharmed. This is exactly what happened, and it meant the end of the rebellion and the restoration of peace between the feuding tribes and the Ruler of Ras Al Khaimah.

After this highly unusual but successful operation, Rashid and I were discreetly informed that we had been recommended for one of the highest military awards for bravery. It was explained that this was in recognition of the fact that we had totally disregarded our personal safety in order to resolve a potentially explosive situation without blood being shed. However, the decision-making politicians in England apparently decided it would not be appropriate in the current sensitive political circumstances to approve bravery awards in a peaceful region that would shortly no longer be under British protection. This decision was confirmed to us in confidence and, although we were both understandably disappointed, we remained proud in the knowledge that we had managed to resolve a potentially dangerous situation peacefully. I am sure there are many other deserving cases that have never been given the credit they deserve, but Sheikh Saqr called for me a few days after the incident and presented me with the most beautiful gold watch I have ever seen.

I recently visited my old camp at Hum Hum with my good friend Dr Saif Baddawi and was delighted to discover that a museum is being built there which will record the military past of the region. After the camp tour, we stopped as usual for a traditional small cup of Arabic coffee, to which it is so easy to become addicted. One middle-aged male civilian who was sitting with us kept staring at me intently, and eventually I asked if I could be of assistance to him. He replied that he was trying to remember where we had met before, but thought it was a long time ago. Suddenly, all became clear. As a youth he had been one of Saif bin Ali's supporters and had witnessed the whole incident. He had seen Rashid and me climbing the hill to begin our long drawn-out negotiations with Saif bin Ali, and our eventual departure with the ringleaders as our prisoners. We now greeted each other enthusiastically with much laughter, like old friends reunited after a long absence. He assured me that the order had been given to fire at us as close as possible in an effort to persuade us not to advance, but he added that, although it was not their intention to shoot us deliberately, they had been told not to worry too much if that did happen. He told me his name was Rashid Ali Al Khatiri, and diplomatically explained that at the time he had been too young to carry a rifle, but the wry smile on his face told me otherwise. He insisted that on my next visit I must call on him and we would meet old members of his tribe who would remember me and the younger ones who would also know all about that historic event that took place on that remarkable day so many years ago. He promised me a warm, friendly reception and, true to his word, that was exactly what I received when I went with him to meet members of his tribe at a grand luncheon.

Not long after the 'Saif bin Ali rebellion' it was once again time for the squadrons to rotate, and this time 'Shiny B' was to be deployed to Masafi in the mountains. During our time at Hum Hum, my squadron had operated well and gained the trust of the local people but it was still very apparent that the mountain tribes were not keen on or receptive to a local military presence. We had been replaced in Hum Hum by A Squadron, commanded by Major John Whitelaw, with Captain Tim Courtenay as his most able 2i/c. Like us, they too spent most of their time trying to keep the 'mountain men' away from their favourite pastime of firing at the Germans at the quarry, and built on the good relationship with Sheikh Saqr that we had established. Sheikh Saqr personally came to see us at Hum Hum before we departed and thanked the squadron for all our efforts, which had helped to restore peace and stability in his state. He assured us that, from then on, the TOS would always be welcome in Ras Al Khaimah. Mission accomplished.

Masafi was considered a good deployment because it was situated in the mountains in the south-east of Ras Al Khaimah, where it was always cooler in

The author in 1960 at a traditional Arab *fuddle* (communal meal). As usual, this armed retainer has his rifle with him.

Scenes from the past:

Above: The first Jashanmal store in Dubai, in 1959.

Below: Dubai International Airport in 1960.

Above: The old Ruler's Palace in Sharjah in 1960.

Below: The spartan conditions of Mirfa tented camp in 1960.

Above: The author leading the guard of honour outside the Ruler's Palace in Sharjah in 1967. On the left of the picture is HH Sheikh Khalid bin Mohammed Al Qasimi, the Ruler of Sharjah, and on the right is HH Sheikh Sabah Al Salim Al Sabah, the Ruler of Kuwait.

Opposite top: HH Sheikh Zayed bin Sultan Al Nahyan (back left) and the Commander of the Trucial Oman Scouts, Col Stewart Carter (second left) in 1960 together with tribesmen and their beloved falcons.

Opposite bottom: A group of newly-commissioned TOS officers in 1968. Seated second left is Sheikh Faisal bin Sultan Al Qasimi, now a prominent UAE businessman and close friend of the author for over 50 years. On his left is Abdul Aziz bin Mohammed Al Qasimi, a brother of the Ruler of Sharjah.

Above: The author on a training exercise in Ras Al Khaimah in 1970, with Ferret armoured cars. With him is signals officer Capt Abdullah, who was on loan from Saudi Arabia.

Left: Ruth Willis, aka 'Miriam, Angel of the Desert' in Ras Al Khaimah in 1970. The girl she is holding was called Shaikha and suffered from TB of the spine. She was a lovely girl, always with a smile. She lived with Miriam until she died shortly after this photograph was taken.

20 - 7 - 1971

The Times Diary

Lonely Shaikh Saqr goes it alone

It was characteristic of Shaikh Saqr bin Muhammad al-Qasim, ruler of the tiny Persian Gulf Shaikhdom of Ras al-Khaymah, that he alone of the seven Trucial rulers should have declined to sign the preparatory agreement to establish a political union.

Saqr is 51 and has for long been regarded as the odd-man-out among the Trucial shaikhs. He is lonely, introspective and highly suspicious of his Gulf neighbours, particularly wealthy Abu Dhabi and minute Fujairah. He has scarcely more confidence in his own population, possibly because he himself came to power through a palace coup in 1948 when he overthrew his father, Shaikh Sultan, and only three years ago he unmasked a plot to depose him.

Ever since the idea of a Gulf federation was proposed at the beginning of 1968, Saqr, whose wall eye gives him a piratical air, has toed an independent line. In 1968 he surprised his neighbours (and the British Government) by proposing to set up a republic in the area embracing the whole of greater Oman—although his republican sympathies are believed to stem mostly from his son, Shaikh Khalid, who was educated at Loughborough.

A year and a half later in Abu Dhabi he broke up a meeting of Gulf rulers, who were discussing the proposed federation, when he staged a spectacular walk-out with Shaikh Ahmed of Qatar. Ahmed was eventually persuaded to leave his yacht and return to the meeting, but Saqr was beyond recall driving across the desert to his stony capital 200 miles away.

With a population only the size of Harpenden (about 15,000) and with Iran laying claim to his off-shore dependencies, the Tumbs islands, Saqr would be unwise to declare UDI. Nevertheless, he likes to feel that with oil prospecting in hand, a large cement plant being built, plans for a commercial television station being discussed, and his own army of about 100 men, the state could survive independently if necessary.

Extract from *The Times*, 20 July 1971.

Below: Letter from the author attempting to correct the errors in *The Times* article.

The Gulf federation

From Lieutenant Colonel D. E. G. Neild

Sir, I write with reference to your recent article in *The Times* Diary (July 20) concerning Shaikh Saqr Bin Muhammad Al Qasmi, the independent Ruler of Ras Al Khaimah. Eighteen months ago, I had the honour of forming His Highness's private army, and feel qualified to explain his recent actions. At the same time I would like to rectify some of the errors in your article.

Shaikh Saqr is, and always has been in favour of a Federation. His son Shaikh. Khalid the Deputy Ruler signed the constitution drawn up by the seven Trucial States deputy rulers and Qatar in Abu Dhabi last October. His Highness has consistently repeated his willingness to join the Federation on those terms.

The new Federation however differs widely from the former. For example: Abu Dhabi and Dubai have more votes in council than the remainder, before it was equal. The Chairman is now for a period of five years, not two years as before. Probably the most important change is that Abu Dhabi and Dubai have the power of veto, never agreed to before. In effect, the other Trucial States rulers have sold themselves out and no longer will have an effective say in the running of their states. Already there are signs of decisions being made in neighbouring states with little or no reference to the Ruler.

I was at a meeting held by the Ruler the day after his decision not to join the Federation attended by over three hundred tribal representatives. After explaining his reasons for his decision he was given the Arab equivalent of a standing ovation—his tribes quite definitely are backing him. Shaikh Saqr will not allow Ras Al Khaimah, so steeped in Arab history to play only a minor part in the future of the Gulf.

As to your article, Shaikh Saqr came to power not by overthrowing his father, who died here peacefully last year, but his father's brother. There is nothing strange in this, five of the present seven Trucial States rulers came to power by coups. The population of Ras Al Khaimah by an official census two years ago was 25,000 but is more like 40,000. The Tumb island problem is indeed a serious one but as Shaikh Saqr says this is a problem for the Arab world not just himself. An off-shore oil strike would be a real blessing for Ras Al Khaimah although it is nothing far short of a miracle to see what has been achieved on such a minute budget. The strength of my army by the way is 250 and not 100 as mentioned.

Anyone who has had the privilege of meeting Shaikh Saqr will realize that he has made his recent decision purely for the good of the people and not for personal or financial gain.

Yours faithfully,
D. E. G. NEILD, Commander,
Ras Al Khaimah Mobile Force,
Ras Al Khaimah,
Arabian Gulf.

Above: The author with Trevor Bevan, Commander of the Ras Al Khaimah Police Force. Taken in 1970 outside the RAK Mobile Force HQ.

Below: HH Sheikh Saqr bin Mohammed Al Qasimi with the author and his wife Eileen in 2006 outside the Palace in Ras Al Khaimah. It was the first meeting between the Ruler and Mrs Neild.

Left: Mohammed bin Abdulla bin Obaid, one of the RAK Police section stationed on the island of Greater Tunb when it was invaded by Iranian forces on 30 November 1971. He is proudly displaying the leg that still bears the scars of the bullet wound he received in action that day.

Right: Hamtoo Abdulla Mohammed, the RAK Signaller stationed on Greater Tunb who informed the author of the invasion over the radio as it was happening. He was the only member of the section who did not receive bullet wounds that day.

Left: Salem Suhail bin Khamis was the RAK Policeman killed in action at the age of 20, defending the Ras Al Khaimah flag during the invasion of the island of Greater Tunb by Iranian forces on 30th November 1971. He is now recognised as the first person killed in action defending the UAE. Salim's body was buried on the island by the fishermen working there before they were forced to leave. Only one photo of Salem exists – this official photo in a police uniform as he joined the Force at the age of 18. From 2015 the date of 30 November has been set as the national Martyr's Day, commemorating all who have given their lives for the UAE.

Opposite: An historic photograph of the leaders of the Emirates after the declaration of the Union at Jumeirah Palace, Dubai, in 1971.

Below: The Union of the seven Emirates is complete with the accession of Ras Al Khaimah, photographed here at the Presidential Palace in Abu Dhabi on 10 February 1972.

From left to right:
HH Sheikh Rashid bin Ahmed Al Mualla, Crown Prince of Umm Al Quwain
HH Sheikh Sultan bin Mohammed Al Qasimi, Ruler of Sharjah
HH Sheikh Rashid bin Saeed Al Maktoum, Vice President of the UAE and Ruler of
         Dubai
HH Sheikh Zayed bin Sultan Al Nahyan, President of the UAE and Ruler of
         Abu Dhabi
HH Sheikh Saqr bin Mohammed Al Qasimi, Ruler of Ras Al Khaimah
HH Sheikh Mohammed bin Hamad Al Sharqi, Ruler of Fujairah
HH Sheikh Humaid bin Rashid Al Nuaimi, Crown Prince of Ajman

The author with Sgt Major Rashid Abdallah Al Shamsi of B Squadron who accompanied the author on the courageous operation that brought a peaceful end to the Saif bin Ali rebellion.

Above: HH Sheikh Saqr bin Mohammed Al Qasimi sharing a private moment with the author in 2002 at the first Trucial Oman Scouts reunion. It was their first meeting for 30 years.

Left: The first Trucial Oman Scouts reunion, which took place in 2002. The photograph of the group was taken at Fort Jahili, near Al Ain.

The author photographed in 2002 with HH Sheikh Sultan bin Saqr Al Qasimi who commanded the RAK Mobile Force after the author left.

The second Trucial Oman Scouts reunion in 2012 at the Camp Hum Hum site.

Above: HH Sheikh Saud bin Saqr Al Qasimi (*centre*) and his son Sheikh Ahmed bin Saud (*left*) welcome the Neild family in the Palace grounds in 2015. With David and Eileen are granddaughters Samantha and Kimberley, daughter Michelle and son-in-law Sean.

Below: The author and his wife Eileen admiring a camel belonging to a member of the ruling family of Ajman.

summer and there was an abundance of clear mountain water to drink. The unspoiled, beautiful Batinah coast was also not too far away, accessible only by a dry river bed (wadi). However, when it did occasionally rain, the wadi would be transformed into a raging torrent, sweeping away anything in its path, including vehicles and people. It was a basic rule never to camp overnight on the river bed itself. Today, a large UAE water company sources its water from this region and a 'Masafi' label adorns all its bottles, something I would never have thought possible in those days.

As already mentioned, many of the tribes throughout the Trucial States were renowned for their long-running feuds, which frequently led to fatalities when they clashed, mainly over boundary disputes. The TOS was frequently involved in dealing with such skirmishes and attempting to find a solution acceptable to all concerned. In the early 1950s, Julian Walker, an energetic young man from the Political Agency in Dubai, had spent many lonely weeks at a time mapping the area and defining borders, and was highly regarded by all the tribesmen he met. His painstaking work resulted in the boundaries generally accepted on the maps of the Emirates today.

On one occasion, soon after our arrival in Masafi, we received reports of shooting near a date garden not far away. The first task on reaching the scene was to establish a 'ceasefire', before investigating the reason for the shooting. Once we had persuaded both sides to stop firing at each other, I was able to talk to all involved and establish the cause of the flare up. On this occasion, it was all about a lone date palm that was claimed by both parties. It was up to me to review the situation, taking into account that there were hardly any defined or agreed borders, and decide on a course of action acceptable to all concerned. Once I had decided on my proposed solution, I asked both parties separately if they were prepared to abide by my independent and neutral decision, and they accepted. I returned to the offending date palm and ordered that it be chopped down, which was duly done. I then explained to the astonished tribesmen from both sides that, as the boundary line was too vague, it was not possible to make an accurate ruling and, by eliminating the date palm once and for all, neither tribe had gained at the other's expense. Both parties found this to be a fair, if rather unorthodox, solution to their dispute and, importantly, no one lost face. Honour was satisfied.

We few seconded British officers were not only looked on as impartial observers by the local people, but were also presumed by the nomadic tribespeople to be doctors. For some reason, they thought that we were capable of curing most ailments, preferably with an injection on which they always insisted. Tablets were fine, but only the insertion of a needle was guaranteed to cure – and the men, I was reliably informed, believed that it also enhanced another part of the body!

One Friday, the Muslim day of rest, Ian Stewart and I were enjoying a relaxing beer in our camp at Masafi when a Land Rover roared up to our Officers' Mess. A very agitated driver leapt out, shouting that he urgently needed a doctor. Ian and I went outside to see what the problem was and, once the poor man opened the back of the vehicle, the situation became very clear. Inside the vehicle were two Arab ladies dressed in traditional black clothing including the burka, and one of them was a young girl who was in the final stages of giving birth. Both Ian and I were bachelors and had no idea what was expected of us, and we were extremely embarrassed to find ourselves in this predicament. I shouted to Ian to go and fetch hot water and towels, which he hurried off to do, grateful no doubt to be away from the front-line action that was developing.

To my amazement, a head began to appear. This, I hoped, was a good sign as my limited knowledge of military first aid had not included any lessons on childbirth. Ian rushed back with a bowl of hot water and towels, which we gave to the older lady as neither of us wanted to get too involved and because we had no idea what to do with the towels and water anyway. For the first and only time in my life, I actually witnessed the miracle of a child being born, which was incredibly special, even though this birth took place in the back of a dusty old Land Rover.

The older lady, who was probably the young girl's mother, took the water and towels, bit the umbilical cord with her teeth and promptly passed the little boy to me to handle while she attended to the new mother. I was terrified in case I dropped this precious little bundle of fun so, making full use of my rank, I promptly passed the responsibility to Ian, which took the smile off his face. We provided a room for the ladies to have some privacy and suggested that they stayed for as long as they needed before hitting the bumpy track again in their well-worn Land Rover, which had clearly seen better days. We could not believe our eyes when, literally a couple of hours later, the happy family emerged and thanked us for our assistance and medical skills, which the proud father insisted had ensured the safe delivery of his wife's first child, who was now sleeping peacefully in a cardboard box. With their thanks ringing in our ears, we watched them set off once again. Ian and I celebrated the discovery our new skills well into the night.

One of my good friends back at TOS HQ in Sharjah was a staff officer named John Pitt. As I recall, we had both read Sands of Arabia, in which Wilfred Thesiger wrote so eloquently about his epic camel journeys and his crossing of the Empty Quarter. John came up with the idea that we should look into the possibility of organising an expedition for the two of us to attempt to retrace the route that Thesiger had successfully taken. This was no flight of fancy and we were absolutely serious about the prospect. John, being a highly efficient and organised staff officer, with all the right connections, would be a huge advantage. We were pleasantly surprised to discover that the military higher command was very supportive, but sadly this was not the case with the politicians. When we submitted our application for the necessary clearance for our venture, it was turned down. The reason given was that there was a delicate political climate in the area at the time, which would not be helped by a couple of British officers wandering around in the desert on some strange adventure that might be thought by some of the countries involved to have a more suspicious aim.

With that disappointing news, John and I had to settle instead for taking our leave in London, which, as it happened, turned out to be a different type of endurance test. It still required a great deal of physical stamina and, although it did not involve the use of camels, it did require us to visit and check out numerous watering holes.

Much as I enjoyed the social whirl in London and elsewhere, financed by the generous hardship allowances I received from the TOS, I was also more than ready to return to our more Bedouin way of life after the hectic pace of my time away from the desert. Back in the Trucial States, the Muslim holy month of Ramadan was always a particularly testing time in the rifle squadrons, as military patrols and operations had to continue as normal. I always made a point of observing the daylight fasting hours along with my soldiers, because I took the view that I could not ask my men to perform duties that would not be a problem for me if I had been eating and drinking. I do admit, however, to frequently breaking the fast with a cold beer rather than a non-alcoholic beverage.

A couple of months after our move to Masafi in early 1969, I was surprised to be informed that HH Sheikh Saqr wanted me to call on him. I received permission from our HQ in Sharjah to proceed to Ras Al Khaimah and all of us were intrigued to learn the reason for his invitation, since 'Shiny B' was no longer located in his territory. The Ruler greeted me warmly and, once again, the

Crown Prince, Sheikh Khalid, and the financial advisor, Tawfiq Abu Khatr, were present, along with the Ruler's personal secretary, Victor (who happened to be the financial advisor's brother). The Ruler brought up the subject of the surprise decision by the British government in January the previous year to hand over the security and foreign affairs of the States to the seven rulers themselves, with the hope of creating a united country no later than December 1971. This was being discussed by everyone and it was no secret that not all the states were enthusiastic about it. This was hardly surprising considering the region's turbulent history, and also that Abu Dhabi and Dubai were the only oil producers and would therefore more than likely expect to have a greater role and prominence in the new formation.

I wasn't really sure where this conversation was heading until Sheikh Saqr informed me he had taken the decision to form a small independent mobile force that would be loyal only to him and Ras Al Khaimah. Abu Dhabi had already gone down this road, with Tug Wilson commanding the Abu Dhabi Defence Force. The presumption was that the TOS and ADDF would merge after 1971 to form a new UAE army.

I knew only too well that the prospect of another independent army would not be well received by our political masters but, at the end of the day, it was for each ruler to decide what he wanted after considering all the available facts. The timing of the British government's unexpected decision had taken all of us by surprise, especially in light of its recent promises not to leave the Trucial States. The announcement had created considerable uncertainty in all seven states and it was hardly surprising that some of them were weighing up options not entirely to the liking of the British government. As Sheikh Saqr continued the discussion, sitting very close to me and talking directly to me, I was certainly not remotely prepared for his next declaration. He informed me that he wanted me to leave the British Army so that I could form and command a Ras Al Khaimah Mobile Force. Sheikh Saqr told me that he had selected me for this role because he had been impressed with how I had handled the recent tribal rebellion and had also received favourable comments about my suitability from Ras Al Khaimah personnel serving in the TOS who he had consulted. To my complete surprise, they had apparently informed the Ruler that, despite my young age, they considered that I was the best suited to be approached and offered the command.

There have been few occasions in my life when I have been at a loss for words, but this was certainly one of them. I think I muttered something about it being a great honour but I would need time to fully grasp the significance of the proposal and consider my future.

To form and command an independent army has to be the ultimate challenge for (and dream of) many professional soldiers, but I had to consider whether I was ready to resign from the British Army, which was my life. I had a British military career ahead of me, probably revolving around the Middle East, with reasonable prospects of future promotions together with the security of a pension at the end of the day. I was reeling from this totally unexpected and incredible offer, and we agreed that I should go away to discuss it with my superiors and return a few days later with my answer.

The Ruler's financial advisor, Tawfiq, walked out with me, telling me in no uncertain terms that he could not believe that I had not immediately jumped at the offer of a lifetime, and he let me know he was not impressed by my attitude. I tried to explain to him some of the major decisions that were facing me and he took me to his office, where he showed me the proposed (extremely attractive) terms and conditions, which included a furnished home and a Mercedes staff car. Although Ras Al Khaimah had been prospecting for oil, there had as yet been no discovery and, as the state had no other major income that I was aware of, I asked Tawfiq how Ras Al Khaimah could even begin to contemplate the formation of an independent army. He replied that they were well aware of the serious financial implications involved, and gave me an assurance that another Middle Eastern country had already guaranteed to provide more than sufficient funds to set up the Mobile Force (RAKMF), but he would not divulge any further details until I had made my decision known.

With my brain playing ping-pong as I weighed up the pros and cons of the offer, I went to inform my CO, Colonel Pat Ive. I was not at all surprised to see his unhappiness at learning that there was a distinct probability of another new military force in the region, and he was even taken more aback at the Ruler's choice of me to command it. We then went to see Julian Bullard, the new Political Agent in Dubai, who was furious to hear my news, as this confirmed his suspicion that Ras Al Khaimah would probably be the most reluctant of the seven States to join the UAE.

Bullard decided to have an audience with Sheikh Saqr in an attempt to persuade him to change his mind or, if that failed, to get him to agree to the secondment of a serving British officer – preferably one with far more experience than me – to take command of the force.

The more I thought about the offer, the more excited I became. I realised that this was a unique, once-in-a-lifetime opportunity, and that I would regret it for the rest of my life if I did not take it. I was young, and keen to continue my military service in the region, but the future of the TOS was not looking good and in all probability it would be incorporated into the new proposed Union Defence Force. Besides, who needed the boring security of a pension anyway?

Unbeknown to me at the time, considerable political dialogue was going on with regard to another independent army being formed in Ras Al Khaimah. Records now available to the public show that the British government had hoped that Sheikh Saqr would turn to General Willoughby, head of the Bahrain-based Military Coordination Committee, Persian Gulf, for advice on the development of his proposed new security force. The British policy at that time was to follow the principle of *festina lente* ('make haste slowly') whereby, although the UK realised that it could not prevent Ras Al Khaimah from procuring imports of modern weapons, it could do everything possible to slow this down and delay the formation of the Mobile Force for as long as possible. Surprisingly, the British government did not voice any objection to Sheikh Saqr's selection of me as commander of his force, perhaps because a precedent had already been set with the recruitment of Tug Wilson to command the ADDF. I now know that I also received the personal support of Julian Bullard, when he wrote that he thought I had 'the qualities to do the job excellently,' and added that in his opinion 'Neild is a man who could serve Sheikh Saqr without losing sight of HMG's interests'.

To the best of my recollection, General Willoughby never contacted me, and the choice and selection of all the necessary weapons and equipment for the RAKMF were made by me with the approval of the Crown Prince. I was also never aware of the British applying the policy 'to make haste slowly' in respect of the RAKMF, and was actually impressed with the speed and efficiency of the (UK) Crown Agents, who delivered our military hardware. I am also grateful for Julian Bullard's complimentary remarks about my suitability to raise and command the Force. They were far more flattering than those of one of my previous COs, who wrote in my annual confidential report 'The men follow Neild, mainly out of curiosity'.

There are volumes of correspondence in the British National Archives related to the problems the Foreign Office envisaged regarding the creation of the RAKMF, and it is clear that they continued to apply pressure through the Political Agent to make Sheikh Saqr think again. Foreign Office officials also put forward the argument that if Sheikh Saqr was determined to have his own military force it should be incorporated into the established Ras Al Khaimah Police. Sheikh Saqr, in his response, pointed out the long-standing disputes between his mountain tribes and the German quarry company, which continued to be a constant obstacle to the future development of the region. He stressed that this was his principal reason for establishing his own military unit.

Interestingly, in October 1969 Sir Alec Douglas-Home, the Shadow Foreign Secretary at the time, raised the issue of the formation of the RAKMF with the government, expressing his concerns that it might 'queer our pitch with Iran'. The official Foreign Office reply to this question, issued on 3rd November, stated that:

> Ras al Khaimah suffers from a good deal of tribal unrest and we were advised by the British Military authorities in the Gulf that a force of the type and size envisaged by Sh. Saqr would not be unreasonably large to maintain internal security in the State. In view of this we raised no objection to the idea in principle even though we knew that might not be very welcome to the Ruler of Fujeirah or, perhaps to Shaikh Zaid of Abu Dhabi.

Bullard wrote to the Political Resident in Bahrain that he believed that Sheikh Saqr seemed sceptical that the UAE would succeed in setting up an effective military force, but if that was achieved he might be willing to convert his Ras Al Khaimah Mobile Force soldiers into policemen. Bullard went on to suggest to the Ruler that a police mobile force based on the Dubai model would be suitable for Ras Al Khaimah, but Sheikh Saqr said he did not think so as he believed that 'every man has his trade, and policeman and soldiers are two different things'. I could not have put it better myself.

Finally, Bullard once again wrote to the Residency informing them that Britain's announcement to withdraw meant Sheikh Saqr considered that he had to guard his state against external threats. Sheikh Saqr told Bullard that, in an ideal world, he would prefer the TOS to continue in its present role beyond 1971, but he was certain that this would not happen. This meant that Ras Al Khaimah would be left exposed and therefore he had to take action to provide his own form of protection for his state. Realising that Sheikh Saqr had made his mind up, Bullard argued with the Foreign Office that Britain 'can not very well stand in the way of such measures as the rulers think it necessary to guarantee their own security after we are no longer prepared to guarantee it ourselves'. Game, set and match to Sheikh Saqr.

Julian Bullard made one final effort to persuade Sheikh Saqr to change his mind about the formation of the RAKMF on 16 November 1969. His report to Weir at the Bahrain Residency two days later makes interesting reading.

> I drove up to Ras al Khaimah on 16 November to speak to the Ruler and his son as authorized in your telegram 157 (not to all). Having evicted Neild from the Majlis [parliament], where he seemed already quite at home, I told Sh. Saqr that I wanted to talk to him on my own initiative and as a friend. He knew we had reservations about his project for a mobile force. Eventually when we saw that his mind was made up, we had told him that we would not stand in his way. Now the time had come to put his decision into effect. Before Saqr did this I wanted him to consider the project again from three points of view. Did he need a mobile force? What would be the effect on his neighbours? And could he afford the cost, especially the running expenses? If Saqr was in any way inclined to cancel or reduce or defer the project, I was ready to help him in the difficulties which would arise with Neild, the Saudis and the supplier firms.
>
> Saqr replied at length, interrupted every few minutes by the ringing of his new toy, a Japanese fake Victorian telephone on an imitation brass stand. He said he had thought about these matters a great deal. He had been Ruler for something like 17 or 18 years (in fact it is 21) and not one of those years had been free from some kind of trouble with the tribes. This was an internal problem and he wanted rid of it. He now faced an external problem too. The British had announced that they were withdrawing. (Saqr incidentally did not speak as if he expected or particularly wanted this decision to be changed.) Ideally the TOS should continue but Saqr was 90% certain that this would not happen. Who would guarantee Ras al Khaimah's security after 1971? At the moment Saqr was hesitating between Iran, as the strongest power in the area, and Saudi Arabia, as his traditional friend. He was also more concerned, even more than before, at the growth of Abu Dhabi. In the circumstances he was certain a mobile force was a necessity. His neighbour

Rulers had accepted the principle of local forces at one of the first meetings of the UAE, and he was only applying the principle. As to the cost he had calculated that he could definitely afford the expense of the first two years, at the end of which Ras al Khaimah's circumstances would have improved. Oil might be found on shore or off shore and business was booming. Every month Saqr was receiving a dozen applications for permission to open shops or businesses in the town and speculators had spent QDR 20 million on land in the area. In any case Saqr would renounce anything rather than his mobile force. He thanked me for my words, which he accepted in the spirit of friendship in which they were offered, but assured me that his mind was made up.

This result was what I had expected after a conversation the previous day with Neild, who told me he had called on Saqr just before signing off from the TOS to check he was not having second thoughts. Saqr had then assured him that whatever other projects he might have to abandon, he was determined to go ahead with the Mobile Force.

I confess I was somewhat amused by Bullard's claim that he had 'evicted me' from the Majlis. I was always present throughout his visits and he had neither the diplomatic nor the martial skill to achieve such an eviction. I can only assume it made him feel better to write it, possibly to impress the Foreign Office personnel to whom he answered.

A further meeting took place between Sheikh Saqr and Julian Bullard, with the Ruler refusing to agree to any of the Political Agent's suggestions, including the offer of a seconded British Army officer to command the Mobile Force. Sheikh Saqr later explained to me that the reason he had declined the offer of a seconded officer was that he was concerned that, if this officer was still a serving member of the British Army, there could easily be a conflict of interest and the man's total loyalty to him as Ruler would be in doubt.

The opinion of most of my brother officers was that it would be unwise for me to resign my commission to take up a position which had no guarantee of long-term employment. I believe it would also be accurate and fair to say that there was a considerable amount of resentment from a few of the more senior, longer-serving TOS officers who, understandably, were far more experienced and qualified than me. I returned to Ras Al Khaimah and informed Sheikh Saqr that I would be honoured to accept his offer and would do my utmost to justify his confidence and trust in me. He was genuinely pleased that I had accepted the appointment. Thus began a very special relationship between us, which lasted for the rest of his long life.

To implement this decision, I wrote my letter of resignation from Her Majesty's Forces which, once the authorities realised that my mind was set to leave the British Army, they had no option but to accept. I made my farewells to my Arab soldiers, who were thrilled to learn of my promotion and the challenge awaiting me in Ras Al Khaimah, and their support meant a great deal to me. In particular, Sheikh Faisal bin Sultan, a son of the ex-Ruler of Ras Al Khaimah, and one of the first TOS Arab officers to be commissioned from Mons Officer Cadet School in England, gave me sound advice and encouragement that helped me enormously. Faisal eventually left the TOS for the ADDF, becoming a major general and Chief of Staff and Chairman of the Court of the Crown Prince (HH Sheikh Khalifa bin Zayed Al Nahyan) before entering the civilian world. He is now a highly respected, successful businessman and our friendship is as strong today as it was 50 years ago. Back in the Officers' Mess, the reaction to my acceptance of my new military role was more reserved. Understandably, a number of my colleagues had considerable doubts about my ability to succeed, as it would be a momentous challenge for anyone, even for an officer with far more experience than me.

Shortly after my decision to accept the offer became known, I was approached by a senior official at the British Political Agency in Dubai. He made it very clear that my loyalty should always remain first to the British government and second to Sheikh Saqr. I will not repeat the exact language of my response, but I made it abundantly clear that I would answer to Sheikh Saqr and my loyalty was to him and him alone. Needless to say, the official was less than impressed with my reply. I realised there and then that I would be wasting my time looking for my name in any of Her Majesty's Birthday Honours lists in the future!

My military career as a regular officer in Her Majesty's Armed Forces was at an end. I would always look back on my service with nostalgia and pride, and I remember with great affection all those with whom I had been fortunate to serve. My time in the TOS had been very special and I realised only too well that this was the reason for being offered the challenging command that was awaiting me. With my ever-faithful orderly Gus at my side, I marched off to Ras Al Khaimah to discover what exciting future lay ahead of us.

SOLDIER OF FORTUNE

The literal English translation of Ras Al Khaimah is 'Head (or Top) of the Tent'. There are several theories to explain the origin of how Ras Al Khaimah came by its name but, to the best of my knowledge, no one can be sure which is correct. I have discussed these various options with a number of educated local historians and there are two that I believe could well be correct. The first possibility is that it was a reference to a prominent mountain feature, similar in appearance to the top of a tent when observed by early sailors from offshore. Another possibility dates back to 1819 and an Italian reference to a Sheikh's tent high above the seashore and clearly visible to passing sailors. Considering the maritime history of Ras Al Khaimah, both suggestions are very plausible.

Archaeological excavations in the area prove that it is one of the few places in the world that has been continuously inhabited since the Late Stone Age more than 7,000 years ago. Records confirm that inhabitants of Ras Al Khaimah travelled to Bombay, China and Zanzibar as early as the tenth century. There are still many historical remnants to be seen, which make it an attractive destination for history enthusiasts.

The town of Ras Al Khaimah, or Julfar, as it was originally called, was during the 14th and 15th centuries, one of the very few established, thriving settlements in the Arabian Gulf, along with Basra, Hormuz, and Manama on the island of Bahrain. The local inhabitants of Ras Al Khaimah were mainly fishermen and pearl divers. However, as already mentioned, cheaper Japanese cultured pearls had flooded the market by the end of the 1930s, which collapsed the demand for natural pearls. With the discovery of oil in the 1950s and 1960s, Abu Dhabi emerged from the shadows. Around the same time, Dubai, with its own smaller oil reserves, grew into a dynamic centre of international trade. Abu Dhabi and Dubai are now the two most prominent and powerful of the seven states and have achieved worldwide recognition for the manner in which they have transformed their humble desert origins into bustling modern cities.

Ras Al Khaimah, without revenue from oil, has taken a different path to its modern development. The magnificent, rugged Hajar Mountains provide a stunning backdrop to the territory and continue to the high peaks at the north of the Musandam Peninsula. Between the mountains and the miles of idyllic, sandy coastline are the fertile agricultural lands that were, in the past, blessed with an abundance of fresh surface and underground water. However, more recently, in common with the rest of the Emirates, population growth has had a serious impact on water reserves, which in some areas have now largely dried up.

When I first took up residence in Ras Al Khaimah, the town was divided by the same sea inlet as it is today, but the inhabitants could only cross from one side to the other by using *abras* (small ferry boats), or alternatively taking the long journey by vehicle on the bumpy, sandy road. Fishing and dhow-building were the main occupations of the people on the coast and, because of the abundance of water available, agriculture flourished in the form of date plantations and various fruit and vegetable farms inland. Old, colourful *souqs* that sold everything needed for the people's frugal lifestyle were also located in the old town on the sea side of the creek. Modern buildings were also beginning to emerge in the new town of Nakheel, situated on the inland side of the creek. The historic fort, which had been the residence of the rulers in the past, was now the home of the local police force and prison. The old watchtowers, originally built on high points along the coast to give early warning of any unwelcome approach by sea, still maintain their lonely vigil.

In 1948, the then Ruler of Ras Al Khaimah, HH Sheikh Sultan bin Salem Al Qasimi, was replaced in a bloodless coup by his nephew HH Sheikh Saqr bin Mohammed Al Qasimi, aged only 28 at the time. Family coups were not unusual and Sheikh Sultan himself had come to power in 1921 by removing his elder brother, Sheikh Mohammed bin Salem, who was the father of Sheikh Saqr. Sheikh

Saqr earned the distinction of becoming the longest-serving ruler in modern times until his death, 62 years later, in 2010. He was personally responsible for overseeing the start of the enormous changes necessary to transform Ras Al Khaimah from a sleepy coastal fishing village to what it has become today. Sheikh Saqr was much loved and respected by all his people, including the few expats who were fortunate to have known him.

In 1969, the local population of Ras Al Khaimah was thought to be approximately 25,000 people. This included a very small group of 'pioneering' expats like me, who had committed themselves to support Sheikh Saqr in developing and improving Ras Al Khaimah. Ted Tucker quietly and efficiently managed to supply electricity to an ever-increasing number of demanding house owners with only basic machinery and a limited budget. Trevor Bevan was the Police Commander with whom I worked closely, and Bob McKay was stationed at the agricultural research station at Dig Dagga. We would all frequently get together on Fridays and Ruth Willis, who worked all hours attempting to establish her medical centre when she wasn't being called out to more remote parts to deliver babies and handle other emergencies, would also join us whenever possible. In my new role as the commander of the newly formed RAKMF, I was privileged to be part of this small group, which made up the Ras Al Khaimah expat community. Fortunately we all got on well together, and we spent a lot of our leisure time exploring the amazing, beautiful contrast of scenery that this very special state had to offer.

For those of you who have never formed a private army, I can assure you it is not for the faint-hearted. It may well sound adventurous, and even glamorous, but when one is actually starting from scratch there are countless vital pieces of the jigsaw to be considered and put together, even before the arrival of the new recruits. For example, a location for the barracks close to the Ruler's home and offices had to be found and approved. Then they had to be built to specifications decided on by a few of us with no previous experience. Equipment, uniforms, weapons, recruitment and logistic requirements, plus a mountain of administrative detail, had to be dealt with, at the same time keeping a close eye on the bottom line of the tight budget. My new command had already been named by HH Sheikh Saqr himself as the Ras Al Khaimah Mobile Force. To the best of my knowledge, this was the first time that the word 'mobile' had been included in the title of a military force, and it accurately described what we were to become.

It was agreed that the Mobile Force would be equipped with the same conventional weapons used by the British forces and the TOS. Our headdress (*shemagh*) would be green and white to highlight the importance of agriculture in Ras Al Khaimah, and the cap badge would be a silver watchtower, as already worn by the Ras Al Khaimah Police, depicting a distinctive historical feature of the emirate.

Sheikh Saqr also took the decision, without consulting me, that I would be promoted to the rank of Lieutenant Colonel. This was a huge promotion for me since I was still only 31 years old, but he considered it was appropriate for the command position that I was to hold. To this day, despite unsuccessful attempts to be called David, my nickname to many is still 'The Colonel'. Indeed, many friends, especially my golfing buddies, have no idea what my true name is, and even my wife Eileen is often greeted by them as 'Mrs Colonel'. I have never used my military title since becoming a civilian, but the nickname has stuck, and I have had to learn to live with it.

I also had to live with frequently being referred to as a mercenary or 'soldier of fortune'. Rather than the true meaning, this description is more likely to conjure up images of Colonel 'Mad Mike' Hoare and his Congo cowboys of the past or others now involved in well-publicised more recent conflicts. The mercenary profession is as old as that other trade, more frequently associated with the fairer sex who prefer, for financial gain, to 'make love not war'. The Romans recruited highly respected professional soldiers (known as 'Wild Geese') from foreign countries to serve as mercenaries in Roman auxiliary units. I also considered myself to be a highly trained, professional soldier who was employed by a friendly country that maintained close ties to the United Kingdom. However, I could not escape the inaccurate views of some outspoken observers who presumed that being a 'mercenary' meant selling oneself for financial gain to become a bloodthirsty killer; nothing could have been further from the truth. I also discovered that I had the dubious honour of being mentioned in Anthony Mockler's 1969 book *Mercenaries*. The fact that I was only a footnote on page 255 and my name was spelt incorrectly did nothing to deter my finger-pointing critics. However, this did not stop me from buying a few copies of the book from Jashanmals in Dubai for family and friends. Fame at last!

Once the British government's initial reluctance to support the RAKMF had been overcome and their stamp of approval eventually, albeit reluctantly, obtained, they did, in all fairness, go out of their way to assist. As a result, the vast majority of vehicles for the RAKMF were purchased through the UK Crown Agents, including three-ton Bedford lorries, Land Rovers, Dodge Power Wagons and Ferret armoured cars. The Dodge Power Wagons were my preferred vehicles for the mortar and machine-gun sections, but the Ferret armoured cars were my pride and joy. The procurement of these vehicles through the services of the Crown Agents would never have been possible had we not received the formal recognition necessary from the British government, which silenced any suggestions that we were not a legitimate force.

The Crown Prince and I worked closely together and gradually, step by step, despite the fact that there was no senior military advisor to whom I could turn for advice, things started to fall into place. We established barracks close to the Ruler's residence, complete with two cannon to display as a military showpiece, together with all the necessary living quarters, storerooms, offices, and most importantly, a secure armoury as well as a couple of prison cells. Once the word was out about the formation of a new army, it was amazing how quickly some extraordinary arms dealers and other dubious merchants appeared. They would offer me wonderful deals with even more fantastic, tempting backhanders, all of which I firmly rejected. These clandestine dealers were another very good reason to support the decision to purchase all our military hardware from the Crown Agents in London. I did inform both the Ruler and the Crown Prince of the lucrative offers that had been made to me and their response was that, provided I selected the best equipment at the most competitive price, there was no problem if it included a 'bonus' for me. The Crown Agents did not operate in that manner, and I continued to rely on my monthly salary for my sole income.

Once the Crown Prince and I had reviewed our budget and agreed on our choice of major items such as weapons and vehicles, we would travel to meet the manufacturers (mainly in the UK) and then purchase the items through the Crown Agents. We were always extremely well looked after and, as potentially valuable customers, we were frequently entertained at the most expensive restaurants and famous hotels in London, which did make our military shopping a most enjoyable experience.

On one occasion, Sheikh Khalid and I had been given the grand tour and we had observed with great interest the Ferret armoured cars that we were keen to purchase. They were put through their paces on various terrains and we could not help but be impressed, so we decided to purchase six, even though we were well aware of the horrendous price of each vehicle and the strain it would put on our tight budget. I could not resist turning to the very professional sales director at the end of the cross-country driving and firing demonstration and saying, 'Wrap them up. We'll take six!'

Meanwhile, the frantic activity continued to ensure that the barracks and everything else was in place in time to receive our first recruits early in 1970. Fortunately, these included some Ras Al Khaimah subjects already trained and serving in the TOS, who had been given permission to transfer to join us. We received enormous assistance and support from the TOS, which enabled us to hit the ground running with a nucleus of well-trained and experienced men. The Ras Al Khaimah Police Force was already well established, with its HQ conveniently based in the historic fort. Gradually we started taking over police duties more suited to the military, in particular patrols into the mountains to monitor the activities and movements of the tribes. Especially important was the attempt to keep the peace between the mountain tribes and the German stone-quarrying company.

This was no easy task, which I already knew only too well from my time with B Squadron when we were stationed at Hum Hum. These 'mountain men' were still extremely volatile and prone to take the law into their own hands, including continuing to shoot at the vulnerable Germans. Although there were plenty of such natural resources to share around, they were not inclined to 'feed' these outsiders. Routine patrolling helped, but decisive action occasionally had to be taken to restore order. On one occasion, there was a serious confrontation when the mountain men threatened to enter Ras Al Khaimah, by force if necessary, to make their long-running grievance known at the Palace itself. Sheikh Saqr was already more than well aware of their dispute with the German company but was always ready to listen sympathetically to them. He would attempt to resolve their demands fairly, but the threat of using force in the town itself was not acceptable. I argued for hours with the leaders to try to persuade them not to take this action, but no settlement was reached. Eventually, I reluctantly had to inform them that, should they cross a specific landmark (a well-defined, isolated small hill on the coast just before Sharm), they would be stopped by military action, which would almost certainly result in fatalities. We then had no option but to take up our position on the hill and from there we watched the tribesmen advance towards us. Fortunately, they stopped metres away from this point when they must have realised that we were serious about carrying out our threat, and retreated back to their mountain homes. When I reported this incident to Sheikh Saqr he was relieved, as we all were, that no lives were lost. He then informed me that the hill in question would thenceforth be known as 'Jebel Neild', but the title deeds were not included! Today Jebel Neild is surrounded by residential properties and it is more in danger of being 'eaten' by property developers than by quarry men or the mountain tribesmen.

My 2i/c, Major Mifta bin Abdulla Al Khatiri, had been transferred from the police and was a wonderful individual with similar skills to those of my old Sergeant Major Rashid, and worth his weight in gold. My junior officer, Sheikh Ahmed bin Humaid Al Qasimi, came from the ruling family and had the benefit of having attended a military college in Egypt for several years. He always did everything with great enthusiasm and was invaluable in dealing with many delicate problems, especially anything connected with administration and logistics, which I would have struggled to resolve. He is now a leading businessman in Ras Al Khaimah, and our friendship is as strong as ever, but it is now my turn to stand to attention and call him 'Sir'!

By this time I had been informed that the funding for the RAK MF had been provided by the government of Saudi Arabia, but it still came as a complete surprise when we received a signals officer from Saudi Arabia as I had not requested anyone. Happily, he brought with him masses of the latest communications equipment, on which we trained our signallers. Another major potential technical problem was thereby solved.

As the size of the force grew towards the target of 300 soldiers, the administrative and manpower workload increased in proportion and I was finding that these tasks were taking up far too much of my already limited time. To overcome this, I recruited ('poached' is probably a more accurate word) Mr Nair, an Indian administrator who had efficiently managed the much larger TOS records department for many years. He had a remarkable memory and could match a soldier's number to his name without referring to any records, an incredible achievement considering the large number of soldiers involved. He was given the rank of captain, which he enjoyed, but which also gave him the authority he needed when dealing with the multitude of soldiers' queries, ranging from leave dates to pay and allowances, along with many other varied problems. His appointment enabled me to devote more time to concentrating on other important priorities, which was essential if the force was to achieve the high standards that I was determined to achieve.

An old favourite saying of mine, repeatedly heard by those close to me, is 'time spent in reconnaissance is seldom wasted'. I have never been impressed by people who are keen to tell you how many long hours they work in a day. In my opinion, what you achieve in the minimum time is the main factor to be considered before a compliment is given.

Somehow, in under three years we managed to equip and train 300 men to form a highly mobile professional force, an achievement in which I took great pride. All credit for this must go to my dedicated team, together with the TOS for their continued assistance. After just two years we laid on our first big military parade. The entire force took part in this, with the Ruler taking the salute while his men and vehicles passed by in front of him. The TOS, as always, came to our assistance on this day by providing their talented pipes and drums band, which added greatly to the occasion. Just about the entire population of Ras Al Khaimah turned out to witness this historic event, and many of them told me afterwards how impressed they were that such a high standard of precision drill had been achieved.

Our next challenge was to demonstrate the military operational skills we had acquired. We had arranged a firepower demonstration in the north of Ras Al Khaimah, after making sure that we had informed the Shehhu and the Hebus high up in the mountains that our intentions were completely friendly. All local dignitaries, including senior TOS officers, were invited to witness the event, which would also give the Ruler and the Crown Prince an opportunity to observe at first hand whether or not my regular glowing progress reports were actually true. The demonstration went off without a hitch and clearly illustrated our ability to deliver a powerful military response in response to any act of aggression, however unlikely. Although our force was small in numbers, we certainly packed a lethal punch and we had demonstrated that we were not to be taken lightly. I was incredibly proud of these visible, practical and effective demonstrations that showed the military capabilities we had achieved in such a short period of time.

On one occasion, I received some curious information about British soldiers who had been sighted in a distant wadi north of Ras Al Khaimah, reportedly asking the few isolated inhabitants in that area to whom they owed their allegiance. I confirmed with Sheikh Saqr that no permission had been requested for any military activity in Ras Al Khaimah so, with his blessing, I set off early the next day with a detachment of my soldiers to investigate. I had two Land Rovers with me, packed with soldiers who were armed to the teeth and as excited as I was to investigate this odd sighting. We entered the stony track of the wadi and the further we travelled along the track the more I realised we were very close to the disputed border with Muscat and Oman. Suddenly, sure enough, we came across a couple of Land Rovers with about seven or eight rugged-looking British soldiers sitting nearby, but there was no indication on their vehicles or their uniforms to indicate to which unit they belonged. They were obviously surprised to see us and were cautious in replying to my friendly greeting. I soon realised, judging by their appearance and attitude, that they had to be an SAS section, and for some inexplicable reason they appeared to be carrying out a discreet border reconnaissance to attempt to define the border and to gauge the feelings of the locals. During our conversation, they commented that Sharjah HQ had not notified them that a TOS patrol would be in the area and they asked me for an explanation why we were there. This made me realise they had not noticed that we were the RAKMF and had instead presumed that we were from the TOS. I made some remark that I would look into it on my return and, having now confirmed their presence and the reason for being there, we made a rapid departure.

I reported my findings to Sheikh Saqr, who immediately demanded an explanation from the Political Agent in Dubai as to why British troops were operating in Ras Al Khaimah without his knowledge. This was to cause a diplomatic incident and eventually an apology was tendered by the Political Agent for the misunderstanding. Meanwhile, I had returned home and, as I sat enjoying a well-earned cold beer, a very agitated TOS major arrived. Pushing his luck, he demanded to know why I had been in Muscat territory pretending to be a TOS patrol, and advised me that he had orders that if his patrol had caught up with me in the wadi they would have arrested me. He eventually calmed down and joined me for a beer, as he now realised that there was nothing he could do about it, at least here in Ras Al Khaimah territory. I also made it very clear that at no time did we attempt to pretend to be anything but an RAKMF vehicle patrol and we were openly displaying our uniforms and vehicle symbols. It transpired that the SAS had radioed Sharjah to find out why they had not been informed of the TOS patrol and eventually someone must have realised it had to be Neild and his Mobile Force. This incident clearly illustrates the point that if I had still been a serving officer in the British forces there would have been a conflict of interest between loyalty to Sheikh Saqr and to the British government. No doubt I would have been ordered not to report the SAS presence to the Ruler. It was fortunate for all concerned that the TOS did not find us and attempt to detain us, as this would have most certainly caused an even greater embarrassing diplomatic problem for the British government.

It would be wrong to give the impression that life in Ras Al Khaimah was all work and no play, because this was certainly not the case. There was a small expat community, as I have already mentioned, which lived together in close proximity and enjoyed each other's company, especially in the cooler months when more wives and children came out to visit.

Trevor Bevan, the police commandant, was affectionately known by his policemen as Abu Chenab ('father of the moustache'), and we worked closely together. Despite being on secondment from the British government, Trevor always had the best interest of Ras Al Khaimah at heart and this loyalty was clearly recognised by Sheikh Saqr, who held Trevor in high regard. I looked on Trevor and his wonderful wife Sheila as family, and I have never forgotten their kindness to me and the memorable times that we spent together. Sheila has written a book about her fascinating life (*The Parting Years*), in which she gives a detailed account of her time in Ras Al Khaimah. Apart from describing life there in those days, she vividly recalls a Christmas Day gathering at their home. Sheila describes how Sheikh Saqr arrived and watched with great interest as the few 'colonials' made fools of themselves playing party games including blind man's buff. The aim of the two blindfolded players is to attempt to hit their opponent as hard as possible with a rolled-up newspaper. Sheikh Saqr, by the look on his face, was highly amused by these antics and clearly thought that, if we were not all totally mad, we were at least eccentric! This incident also clearly illustrates the very close ties our small community had with His Highness (as, indeed, we did with the rest of the ruling family).

In 1955, the British government had established an Agricultural Experimental Farm at Dig Dagga, just outside Ras Al Khaimah city. Robert Huntington, with his wife Jill, carried out trials to find suitable crops that could eventually be grown in the area on a commercial scale. In subsequent years other agriculturists continued their early efforts at the farm, including a great character named

Ted Morgan. On his retirement, Robert and Margaret McKay arrived at Dig Dagga. Robert was also a dedicated agriculturist and was responsible not only for promoting the modern agricultural potential of the area but also for teaching the local people the necessary skills to enable them to establish their own viable gardens.

It was Robert's initiative that led to the arrival of a DC-7 at Dubai Airport with a cargo of two bulls and 28 pedigree Friesian heifers (all in calf) on 20 December 1969. Our small community made regular visits to see how the precious herd were coping with their new surroundings and the heat. It was apparent that they had adjusted well, much to the relief of Robert and his dedicated staff. By June 1970, the cows had all produced their calves, and green-and-white cartons of fresh Dig Dagga milk appeared for the first time in the local shops. This was a truly incredible achievement that paved the way for the start of commercial dairy farming throughout the region. I will always remember the McKay family with great affection and the vital role Robert played in the advancement of crops and livestock. I will also never forget their warm hospitality, especially the annual Christmas carol service and memorable New Year's Eve parties that they always hosted. Fortunately, fresh milk was not the only beverage on offer for consumption on those occasions.

By the mid-1960s, oil was flowing in great abundance from offshore fields, not only in Abu Dhabi but in Dubai as well, resulting in rapid commercial development, and a significant increase in the number of expats living in those areas. However, in Ras Al Khaimah our small, close-knit community still enjoyed our more laid-back, isolated lifestyle. Tarmac roads were being built at an incredible pace in the oil-rich states, but for us it was still a desert track back to Ras Al Khaimah from the big cities or along the beach and seashore, depending on the tides.

It was around this time that Ruth Willis arrived to develop a new medical centre in Ras Al Khaimah. Ruth was a very well-qualified nursing sister who had already spent two years in Aden, but that experience did little to prepare her for the post for which she had volunteered. At her interview in London, Ruth had been advised to read two books by the author Hammond Innes, who had visited the Trucial States ten years earlier. These two books, she was assured, would provide her with all the background she required and prepare her for her new posting. The first book, *Harvest of Journeys,* included approximately half a page on Ras Al

Khaimah, and the other recommended reading, *The Doomed Oasis,* was a novel, although in fairness it was dedicated to the Trucial Oman Scouts!

Ruth has shared with me her first impressions of the hospital in Ras Al Khaimah. 'Pills were handed out or the lucky few got an injection. There were bottles of disinfectant in unlabelled fizzy drink bottles and three syringes with about ten really blunt looking needles. Fortunately there was some emery paper as well to sharpen them up'. From this less-than-basic start Ruth established a hospital to be proud of, and very many Ras Al Khaimah subjects were brought into the world by this incredibly brave and caring woman. On her first morning at work, Sheikh Saqr's elderly father visited the clinic and Ruth was introduced to him as Miss Willis. He decided that Miriam would be a more suitable name for her and thus she was known from that day on. She deservedly won the respect of everyone and would even venture high into the mountains, on foot, to treat people in those remote isolated areas.

Another prominent member of our exclusive group was the aforementioned Tim Ash, who had served with distinction for many years as Desert Intelligence Officer in the TOS. Tim was not that keen on our social life, preferring instead to spend his time mainly with the mountain tribes. He built up a well-justified reputation for his ability to converse with them and, most importantly, gained their trust. He frequently managed to defuse potentially explosive incidents, usually between the mountain tribes and the Ruler, or the companies that worked below them that were involved in the quarry excavation. Tim was asked by Sheikh Saqr to stay on after the merger of the TOS into the Union Defence Force in 1971, and time and again proved how valuable his presence was for all sides when there were sensitive issues to be resolved. With his close bond with the local tribes, Tim became known as 'Ash of Ras Al Khaimah', a fitting and well-earned title.

Both Tim and Ruth had a special relationship with the 'mountain tribes', and there is a romantic ending to their long association with the people of the area. In November 1977 they were married at the former Political Agency in Dubai. This was followed by a traditional ceremony high up in the Hajar Mountains, attended by large numbers of the Shehhu and Hebus mountain tribes and celebrated with much dancing, feasting and volleys of rifle fire which, for a change, were not aimed at the quarry company below. The mountain honeymoon which followed between 'Ash of Ras Al Khaimah' and 'Miriam the Angel of the Desert' was a fitting final act and, to this day, these two outstanding individuals are remembered with great affection and gratitude by the people of Ras Al Khaimah.

I had been informed that a suitable bachelor home would be built for me and, while this was being constructed, I lived in a small flat with very basic furniture. There were only two chairs for visitors but Gus had found a couple of fruit crates that were also used if necessary to make our visitors more comfortable. Once my promised house was completed, I was more than ready to receive visitors and many took up the offer. The property was a two-bedroom, two-bathroom bungalow, which provided me with an ideal bachelor home, complete with decent servant's quarters (at last) for Gus and a newly acquired cook, about whom Gus was not amused. I explained to Gus that having a separate cook would give him more time off and also give my stomach a break from his cooking (which had never improved; in fact it had deteriorated), but he was not easily persuaded. Somewhat reluctantly, he did eventually accept the domestic change in our household and his smile returned. An uneasy truce between the two of them was established, but I don't think Gus ever truly forgave me for bringing an 'intruder' into his kitchen.

In his usual caring way, Sheikh Saqr was one of the first to come and check out my new bungalow to make sure that all was satisfactory and to my liking. By this time I had established a close working relationship with him and I looked up to him, not just as my employer, but with genuine affection.

Sheikh Khalid, the Crown Prince, frequently popped into my home and we began to spend more social time together, especially in the evenings and on Fridays. Sometimes we would go water-skiing on the magnificently protected lagoon where the sea was usually like glass, which enabled us both to become proficient at the sport. On other occasions, we would head out to sea on a dhow to go fishing in locations teeming with so many fish that even I could not fail to catch them. We would often trawl for tuna or small shark using a bigger hook and on one occasion, by total chance, we hooked a sailfish. The entire crew plus the Crown Prince and I became very excited and, covering our hands with cloth for protection, we eventually reeled the very irate sailfish alongside the dhow while it continued to fight strongly. This wonderful fish was far from exhausted and I had visions of Sheikh Khalid, who was enthusiastically in total charge of the operation, being stabbed by the impressive and highly dangerous nose spear, which had already come perilously close to him. To ensure the safety of the Crown Prince, I grabbed my 9 mm Sterling sub-machine gun and very unsportingly shot the unfortunate sailfish several times in the head. Hardly surprisingly, we were then able to haul the fish on board without a struggle, and I was spared the embarrassment of having to report to the Ruler that his son had been seriously injured, or worse, by a sailfish.

Sheikh Khalid was also keen to take an active interest in sport and I suggested that he should try to take up tennis. It was always a problem to attempt any physical exercise in the heat of the summer months but, in addition to that constraint, we had another obstacle to overcome – we did not have a tennis court! Once Sheikh Khalid had shown his willingness to take up tennis, he agreed to the building of a court in front of my house, complete with floodlights to allow us to play in the cool of the evening. He quickly became a keen player and we spent many happy hours, with the local community joining in as well. We started the 'prestigious' Ras Al Khaimah Tennis Championships, open only to bona fide residents, who competed fiercely for the coveted title. Modesty prevents me from naming the first men's singles champion! My old house and tennis court are still there to this day, but are sadly no longer the happy meeting point that was so special all those years ago.

My parents came out from England for Christmas in 1970 and thoroughly enjoyed the visit. I have fond memories of them meeting the Ruler. I had briefed them both on the protocol of the do's and don'ts, but mother was so excited by it all, especially when His Highness invited her to sit next to him, that it was all forgotten. She chatted away to him as only the Welsh can, totally ignoring the fact that he could not understand a word she was saying, and he would answer her in Arabic while telling me to leave them alone because no translation was necessary. They got on like a house on fire and after that meeting Sheikh Saqr would always ask me how my mother was and to be remembered to her.

Another visitor to Ras Al Khaimah was Peter Snow, a British TV news reporter. He came out in February 1970 to make a film on the State, with particular emphasis on the Mobile Force and the Ruler's reasons for forming it. Peter stayed with me during his visit and I found him to be a fascinating house guest, full of wonderful stories from his travels and experiences around the world. The interview with Peter and myself, including his meeting with the Ruler, also contained footage of how Ras Al Khaimah looked back in those days. The programme was aired at peak time on ITN and generated huge interest, which certainly brought Ras Al Khaimah to the attention of a larger audience. The interview and old footage are now available on YouTube and I am astonished at the number of people who still continue to view this old documentary.

It was also quite normal for my old friend Peter Molins from London to make a sudden appearance. The first time he popped in for just a couple of days, but it gave him sufficient time to teach Gus how to make a Bloody Mary to his very high standards. Only when he considered that Gus was sufficiently well trained in this complicated cocktail-mixing skill, and Gus had satisfied Peter with his efforts, did Peter go off once more on his travels.

I made several 'shopping trips' to England with the Crown Prince to purchase military equipment. However, on one occasion I accompanied Sheikh Saqr himself on a visit to the UK. We were staying at the Inn On The Park hotel and His Highness especially enjoyed watching all the various activities taking place in Hyde Park from his balcony. He showed great interest in the kite flying, and we took plenty of kites back to Ras Al Khaimah, though I cannot recall ever seeing any of them being flown there.

The day before we were due to return to Ras Al Khaimah, Sheikh Saqr informed me that he wanted to go shopping and I was to accompany him. In the Rolls-Royce on the way to Harrods, His Highness informed me that he wanted to purchase some clothes for the female members of his family. This did rather take me by surprise, as women and wives were not subjects that were normally mentioned in such a conservative culture. On arrival at the well-known store, we found our way to the ladies department with Sheikh Saqr appearing quite unaware of, or probably not bothered by, the looks he was receiving due to his traditional Arab form of dress. As he wandered around the ladies department, Sheikh Saqr suddenly spotted in a glass display cabinet a mannequin wearing a trouser suit, which was very fashionable in those days. He turned to me, said that the outfit was exactly what he had been looking for and asked me to call the assistant. I explained to the sales lady that His Highness was interested in the trouser suit on display and I then had to translate back to Sheikh Saqr to enquire what size and colour he required. He looked around at the rest of the staff standing nearby and then pointed to one of the lady assistants and said 'that size'. That answered the first question, and when His Highness was asked what colour he would like, he replied 'white'. All appeared to be happily resolved, until His Highness told me that he would take 12 trouser suits, all in white and all the same size. I duly translated this request to the astonished assistant and it really set the tongues wagging among the large group of assembled curious onlookers. I paid for the goods in cash (as we had no credit cards in those days), and we later returned to the limo, where our purchases had been delivered. On the way back to the hotel, I could not resist asking Sheikh Saqr why he had bought 12 outfits of the same design, colour and size. He reminded me that, as they were for the female members of his family, he knew that the only way to avoid arguments between them was to treat them all the same. He explained with a smile that in this way it would keep all his female relatives happy and there could be no cause for jealousy. He assured me that this was the only way to treat family and that I should remember it for the future. This strategy may well have worked for Sheikh Saqr and his female relatives, but there is no way the four female members of my family today would accept it!

Towards the end of 1969, Sheikh Saqr visited Iran for a meeting with the Shah in an attempt to resolve the dispute over the Tunb islands. Nothing of any consequence was achieved, with both sides maintaining positions that did not allow for a settlement. On his return, Sheikh Saqr told me that the Shah was sending a consignment of weapons to Ras Al Khaimah, which we both hoped would be of immense benefit. I was more than a little surprised, and curious to learn more about this apparently generous gesture. The weapons duly arrived, but they were old and used, and with an unusual calibre of ammunition that was not available in the Gulf, so they were of no practical use. When I reported my findings to His Highness, he was certainly not amused but he then informed me that he had also received a number of boxes from the Shah containing little black eggs which tasted very salty. Sheikh Saqr no doubt realised perfectly well that caviar was a delicacy and that the Iranian variety was considered the finest, but it was not to his liking and he asked me if I would like them. I immediately expressed my interest and, to my delight, Sheikh Saqr had the boxes sent over to my house; I dined on the most unbelievable Beluga caviar for some considerable time. The boxes all bore the personal crest of the Shah and, on the rare occasions when I have been offered caviar since, I can say in all honesty that none has ever remotely come close to the flavour and texture of those little salty black eggs that I enjoyed thanks to him.

In July 1970 the Sultan of Oman was overthrown by his son, Qaboos bin Said, and Sheikh Saqr announced soon afterwards that he intended to pay a courtesy visit to Muscat to congratulate the new Sultan. It was agreed that the Crown Prince and the Ruler's financial advisor, together with me and an armed escort from the RAKMF, would accompany the Ruler on the visit. It was also decided that we would make the long journey in a convoy of Land Rovers, crossing from Ras Al Khaimah to the Batinah coast and then down to Muscat. This was an unusual decision, but Sheikh Saqr stated that he wanted to see the Batinah coast again as well as some other parts of the coastal region that none of us had seen before. It took us several days to complete the journey, camping out each night on the sparsely populated coast. Every night we sat around a campfire, listening to Sheikh Saqr telling us stories from his youth and reminding us of the importance of establishing a more cordial relationship with the new Sultan. Despite the fact that I personally drove His Highness throughout our long journey on bumpy, back-breaking tracks, he was always relaxed and he obviously enjoyed the experience. He was also quite content to put up with our basic ablution and sleeping arrangements. Even the irritating presence of persistent flies during the day and hungry mosquitoes at night did not bother him, and he remained in good humour at all times. Along the beautiful sandy coastline we would come across small isolated fishing communities and stop and greet them. Most fishing was done in small boats made from date palms with room only for the fisherman himself. He would sit in this flimsy craft, half submerged, and catch sufficient fish for his family and a few to sell. I did try, much to the amusement of Sheikh Saqr and the others, to attempt to paddle one of the little fishing boats out to sea but it was a skill I did not master. Sitting in this craft with seawater lapping around my waist was an odd sensation, especially when I noticed several highly venomous yellow-and-black banded sea snakes that appeared to be heading in my direction. In record time, I somehow made it back to the shore, where the local fishermen assured us that the sea snakes were not aggressive and rarely attacked anyone. My soldiers, in particular, were not overly impressed by my actions to put as much distance as possible between me and the advancing sea snakes. They found the episode hilarious and made sure that, on our return, all and sundry were told of my 'heroic antics'.

Prior to this journey, I had heard many incredible stories about how the old Sultan had ruled his subjects in a manner more in keeping with medieval times, and was excited at the prospect of seeing Muscat myself for the first time. A joke was doing the rounds that there was a sign at the entrance to Muscat advising travellers to put their watches back 500 years. The town itself had a surrounding wall with an entrance that opened at dawn and closed at sunset. After dark, all the people in the city had to carry a hurricane lamp if they wanted to go anywhere, which was unlikely, as there was basically nowhere to go. It was also decreed by the old Sultan that any of his subjects wishing to purchase a generator, even for domestic use, had to submit a written request to him. The Sultan would eventually consider the request and, if approved, the applicant would receive the necessary clearance, signed by the Sultan himself. No wonder his overthrow by his son was received by Omanis with great rejoicing, with the hope that they too would begin to benefit from the amenities that were now enjoyed by their neighbours across the border.

We were accommodated in a very basic government guesthouse, and I quickly gained the impression that the previous Sultan did not go out of his way to make his visitors too comfortable in case they overstayed their welcome.

The four of us were introduced to Sultan Qaboos at a special audience, where he thanked us for making the long journey and stressed the importance of the historical and geographical links that the two countries shared. I was very keen to meet the new Sultan as he had been trained at Sandhurst, been commissioned and had served for a while in the British Army before returning home to Oman. Once his father realised that his heir was planning to bring Oman into the 20th century, he had his son placed under house arrest. Sultan Qaboos managed to overthrow his father, who subsequently lived in exile in London, spending the last two years of his life at the Dorchester Hotel, a far cry from the basic living conditions he had imposed on his subjects.

Sultan Qaboos seemed somewhat surprised that I was a member of Sheikh Saqr's official party and we talked for a considerable time together. He was extremely interested to learn more of the future of the Trucial States when Britain would relinquish her protection at the end of 1971 and what would be the fate of the TOS.

We had dinner with the Sultan that evening, but at the end of the meal Tawfiq (the financial advisor) and I were asked to leave. This was when the real discussions took place, privately between the two rulers, and, although I was never told in detail what was discussed, I do know the meeting lasted until the small hours of the next morning. This was really no surprise, considering the volatile history between the Sultanate and Ras Al Khaimah, and I am sure they had a great number of outstanding issues, including boundaries, that needed to be addressed.

Tawfiq and I made our way back to the room we were sharing, where we were visited by an aide of the Sultan, who said he had come to see if we were comfortable. He then proceeded to take a huge wad of US $100 notes out of his pocket and, while apologising profusely, explained that there had not been time since the coup for suitable items to be obtained as gifts for their honoured guests. He continued that he hoped we would not be offended to be offered cash instead of a specific gift. Before I could give an assurance that absolutely no offence would be taken at this generous gesture, Tawfiq rejected the offer. He pompously proclaimed that we had not come to Muscat looking for money, and there was no way that we would accept any. When I looked at the cash the aide was holding, I estimated that there must have been several thousand dollars for each of us in his hands. In 1970, this was a small fortune from my perspective. I still wake up at night thinking about that event and plotting my revenge on Tawfiq for his mind-boggling decision. To add insult to injury, I have only recently discovered that Tawfiq is today one of the wealthiest Arabs in the world and lives in Monte Carlo, with a personal fortune reputed to be several billion US dollars. To this day, I ask myself where I went wrong!

We returned to Ras Al Khaimah, with Sheikh Saqr informing us that the long journey had been very worthwhile and much appreciated by the new Sultan. I frequently think back to that epic drive along the Batinah coast and remember not only the time spent with Sultan Qaboos but also the very special days with Sheikh Saqr.

LONG FAREWELL TO RAS AL KHAIMAH

On 24 January 1968, the British Prime Minister, Harold Wilson had announced that the UK would end its treaty relationship with the Trucial States, along with Bahrain and Qatar, by December 1971, which confirmed recent articles in the British press.

Back in 1952, a Trucial States Council had been formed, and Sheikh Saqr was elected as its (revolving) chairman in 1966. One delicate topic that this body had to address was how to achieve a closer relationship between the seven States, but little progress had been made, mainly due to the reluctance of the more conservative Sheikh Shakhbut, the Ruler of Abu Dhabi, to participate in such a venture. With the accession of his brother Sheikh Zayed in August 1966, this all changed. Sheikh Zayed realised the importance of the unity of the seven States and believed that the wealth of Abu Dhabi should be used to the benefit of all.

On 18 January 1967, George Thomson, the British Minister of State at the Foreign Office, announced in the House of Commons that it was 'in the mutual interest of the UK and the Rulers … that we should continue to carry out our obligations to the Trucial States'. Despite this reassurance, rumours had begun to circulate that Britain was considering giving up its protective role, which may well have been one of the reasons behind a later visit to the region by Goronwy Roberts, who replaced Thomson at the Foreign Office. In November 1967, he visited Iran, Saudi Arabia, Abu Dhabi and Dubai and it is a matter of public record that on this trip Roberts reassured all the rulers about Britain's commitment to the Gulf and stated that 'Britain will stay in the Persian Gulf as long as necessary to maintain peace and stability'.

Meanwhile, back in London Harold Wilson's government was fully occupied with an economy that was in freefall. On 18 November 1967, the government announced the devaluation of the pound by just over 14% in a desperate attempt to stem the outflow of remaining foreign currency reserves. On 9 January 1968, the *Daily Express* led with an exclusive report that the decision had been taken to bring home all forces stationed in the Gulf and the Far East. This was confirmed two weeks later by a statement from an embarrassed 10 Downing Street, which added that the planned exodus of military personnel would be completed by the end of 1971. Less than two months after his first visit, Roberts had the difficult task of returning to the region to confirm Britain's withdrawal three years later. Only in Baghdad and Teheran was the news of this sudden reversal of British policy extremely well received.

This announcement of the timescale for the withdrawal of British forces came as a complete surprise to the Rulers, considering the reassurances they had only recently received from senior British government figures. It most certainly came as a bolt out of the blue to us British officers who were serving with the TOS at the time, and we felt let down and humiliated by our political masters. It is very clear from government papers now available that HMG had been planning for a federation of the States for a considerable time, and only brought forward the intended date for policy changes because of the various problems affecting the UK economy.

Some fascinating details that provide further background to these events can be found in the extracts of the diary of Donald Hawley, who was the Political Agent in Dubai from 1958 to 1961. I knew Donald quite well and I see from his book *The Emirates: Witness to a Metamorphosis* that he was well aware of the various developments that were being planned for the Trucial States. On 1 October 1959, he wrote that Sheikh Saqr of Ras Al Khaimah had told him that 'He had heard rumours that HMG had agreed with Iran to withdraw from the Gulf in 15 years. I assured him they were not true.' As we now know from actual events, this 'rumour' was accurate and the predicted date for the withdrawal was out by only a couple of years. Hawley also wrote, on 22 January 1960, that 'Sh Saqr of Sharjah came to lunch in very good form – and I mentioned the advantages of some sort of federation. I do not want to force the pace, but do want to leave the thought with the Rulers and see whether in due course the seed takes.' It would be hard to accept that a Political Agent would have brought up the idea of a federation with a ruler without the prior approval and knowledge of Sir William Luce, the Political Resident in Bahrain, and indeed the British government in London. Luce wrote to Stewart Crawford, FO Assistant Under-Secretary for the Middle East, on 27 May 1964 that 'Federation of the Trucial States is an important aim of HMG's policy.' Patrick Gordon Walker, the Foreign Secretary, wrote to the Prime Minister on 18 December 1964 that 'One essential part of the process of modernization is the federation of the small Trucial Sheikdoms'. It is now apparent that the British government had been working on the 'federation' policy well before the January 1968 announcement of the withdrawal of military personnel from the Gulf. It also explains why HMG was so actively involved and used all its influence to ensure the removal of the previous Rulers of Sharjah and Abu Dhabi, who they considered to be major obstacles to achieving this intended federation.

On 18 February 1968, just over a month after the sudden British announcement, Abu Dhabi and Dubai formed an alliance and invited the other States, including Bahrain and Qatar, to join. The proposed amalgamation was supported by Jordan, Kuwait and Saudi Arabia, but was fiercely condemned by Iran. This was hardly surprising as Iran laid claim not only to Bahrain but also to Abu Musa Island, which belonged to Sharjah, and the Greater and Lesser Tunb islands, which belonged to Ras Al Khaimah.

By the time I arrived to take up my new role as Commander of the Ras Al Khaimah Mobile Force in late 1968, there had been frequent urgent meetings between the nine rulers that had resulted in them all signing a document committing them to work towards unity between the nine states, known as the Dubai Agreement. The harmony of this agreement was short-lived, however, with some of the bigger and more influential states proposing greater control and power over the smaller states – and this latter group included Ras Al Khaimah. From the outset of the talks, Sheikh Saqr had stressed the importance of parity for all, regardless of size and wealth. Historically, the Qawasim ruling families had been far more powerful than the ruling families of the other states, so accepting a lower status was unthinkable to them. They argued that all states in the proposed federation should have equal voting rights. Sheikh Saqr famously stated at the start of one meeting that, 'the nine Rulers [had] arrived as equals and that [was] the only way forward. This [was] not for negotiation.'

At a meeting in October 1969 attended by the rulers of all nine states, remarkable progress towards the federation was achieved when a resolution was passed giving all states equal representation. Sheikh Zayed of Abu Dhabi was to be the first President and Sheikh Saqr of Ras Al Khaimah was unanimously nominated as Vice President. However, Sheikh Saqr explained that he would have to decline the appointment because he did not feel that he would be able to devote the time necessary to carry out the demanding role that the position would require.

The meeting entered a second day, which was apparently interpreted by some observers as a cause for concern. In fact, a great deal had been achieved at the meeting and there were now only a few relatively minor obstacles remaining. James Treadwell, the Political Agent in Abu Dhabi, requested permission to address the meeting and he read out a statement from Sir Stewart Crawford, by now the Political Resident for the Gulf, based in Bahrain. The statement basically expressed dismay at the failure of positive developments and suggested that the nine rulers were making 'poor efforts'. To deliver such critical comments to this prestigious group was, in my opinion, an appalling diplomatic blunder by the British government representative, and it took the rulers completely by surprise. The rulers of Qatar and Ras Al Khaimah walked out of the meeting and an apology was demanded by the remainder. In their eyes, HMG was leaving the Gulf States to fend for themselves because that suited it, and proceeded to severely reprimand the rulers for not resolving their long-standing differences as rapidly as the British wanted, even while they were making progress.

On 11 May 1970, the UN Security Council voted in favour of Bahrain becoming an independent sovereign state, and full independence was achieved on 14 August 1971. During these independence negotiations, there was considerable surprise that this proposal was accepted without objection by Iran, which had always claimed sovereignty over Bahrain. This led many to believe that Iran had struck a discreet deal with the British government, and that it would give up its claim over Bahrain without a struggle in return for assistance from HMG over the disputed Abu Musa and Tunb islands. On 3 September 1971, Qatar followed Bahrain in becoming an independent state. And then there were seven.

I much appreciated the fact that Sheikh Saqr and the Crown Prince made a point of frequently informing me of any developments or lack of progress regarding the negotiations about the formation of a federation, and from early

1971 I was present at many of the meetings that were held in Ras Al Khaimah. It soon became apparent that, in addition to the main subject concerning the whole question of a future federation, the dispute over sovereignty of the Tunb islands was also under discussion. In an attempt to achieve further progress on these issues the British government, now led by Ted Heath, brought Sir William Luce out of retirement and sent him to make frequent visits to the various rulers in what today is called 'shuttle diplomacy'.

Abu Musa and the Greater and Lesser Tunb islands are located at the entrance of the Strait of Hormuz, which is described as the world's biggest oil highway. Although Greater Tunb is only approximately ten kilometres long, and the uninhabited, barren Lesser Tunb only two, the occupation of these islands could enable Iran at any time to threaten to cut off the shipping lines, which would cause serious international economic problems. It soon became obvious that Iran, probably with the tacit cooperation of the UK, was determined to take possession of the Abu Musa and Tunb islands – by negotiation, if possible, but if necessary by force. Luce made very clear to Sheikh Saqr and no doubt also to Sheikh Khalid, the Ruler of Sharjah, that generous compensation would be offered by Iran, including the possibility of a share of any future oil revenues that might be generated from the area around the islands. Sheikh Saqr consistently stated that he was not interested in any of the proposals, and made it abundantly clear that he was not prepared to enter into any form of negotiation regarding the future of the Tunb islands. I vividly remember one meeting where Sheikh Saqr made an emotional statement to a visiting British delegation telling them that he and his family had walked on the islands and that his children and their children would also set foot on them because they belonged to Ras Al Khaimah.

The Tunb islands of Ras Al Khaimah had been at the centre of an international dispute with Iran for a very long time. This situation had been made more complicated by the fact that in the past the Qawasim tribe had lived and traded on both sides of the Straits of Hormuz. In 1904, a European, Monsieur Dambrain, the Director of Persian Customs, visited Greater Tunb and not only replaced the Qawasim flag with a Persian one but also installed two Persian Customs guards. (Reza Shah changed the country's name from Persia to Iran only in 1935.) HMG took this serious incident up with Teheran and a few days later, at British insistence, the Persian flag was lowered and the two guards withdrawn. This positive action clearly demonstrated that the British government was in no doubt that the sovereignty of the Tunb islands belonged to Ras Al Khaimah. In 1914, once permission had been obtained from the Qawasim ruler, the British built a 24-metre white lighthouse on Greater Tunb, powered by gas and serviced by the Middle East Navigation Aids Service. I had visited Greater Tunb on several occasions, and the small fishing community that lived there, who I met, clearly owed their allegiance to Ras Al Khaimah.

The intense pressure applied on Sharjah and Ras Al Khaimah to reach a settlement with Iran over the future of the islands also made the establishment of a federal union of the seven States even more critical. Time was rapidly running out for the British government to hand over protection of the Trucial States at the end of 1971 and it was understandably presumed that a United Arab Emirates would be a more powerful and effective entity to stand up to the increasingly aggressive attitude of Iran.

Throughout this turbulent period of hectic and demanding negotiations, Sheikh Saqr remained as calm and composed as he had always been and my admiration for him increased even more. He still devoted as much time as necessary to dealing with the more mundane, day-to-day problems of the State while patiently explaining to his people the difficulties that were to be faced when the planned Union was formed.

During all the discussions and meetings over the formation of the Union, Sheikh Saqr had consistently appealed for equal rights for all the States, irrespective of their size and wealth. The Ruler of Ras Al Khaimah had maintained this position because of his concern for the long-term future of all the territories, and not in any way due to a falling out with his fellow rulers. In fact, I personally witnessed on numerous occasions a clear atmosphere of friendship and mutual respect when other rulers called on him. It therefore came as a bitter blow when, on 18 July 1971, the rulers of the other six Trucial States signed an agreement to establish the United Arab Emirates. The agreement included a provision that allowed for the other member of the family, Ras Al Khaimah, to sign the declaration at a later date.

In the months that followed the signing of this agreement, there were frequent internal accusations blaming Sheikh Saqr for not signing the agreement, and urging him to reconsider. It came as no surprise when an article appeared in *The Times* newspaper in the UK reporting that Sheikh Saqr had walked away from the other six States and giving false and misleading reasons for him doing so. The article made my blood boil as it was grossly unfair, and I decided to write to the editor in the hope that the pen would prove mightier than the sword. I was pleasantly surprised to see that my letter was published, but the accusations persisted and, apart from releasing some of my pent-up steam, my letter achieved nothing worthwhile. I do remember with great amusement telling a few friends at the time that I had had a letter published in *The Times* at my first attempt, as I knew some of them had been trying for years without success to have a letter published in that renowned newspaper.

The day after the other six States signed the agreement to form the UAE, Sheikh Saqr called a meeting in Ras Al Khaimah attended by all the most influential tribal members and leading businessmen of the community. I was allowed to attend, but was told quite firmly by Sheikh Saqr that I was to keep a low profile and on no account to get involved in the debate. It was a great privilege that I was even allowed to witness the proceedings, which at times were quite volatile. Some attendees were in favour of joining the Union immediately, with others wanting to negotiate more equal terms, and a minority in favour of total independence. The independence lobby was probably pinning its hopes on the (American) Union Oil Company, which had been drilling initially on land and now offshore. The news about offshore oil had previously sounded promising, but by this stage the prospects of the long-awaited 'bonanza' were looking more and more remote. At the end of the meeting, Sheikh Saqr carefully explained his reasons for not signing and received a standing ovation from the vast majority who supported his action. He most certainly had not decided to go it alone, as reported in *The Times*, but was still holding out for full equality.

By mid-1970, we in the RAKMF had achieved all our targets and had a fully operational force of close to 300 trained men in place. This in itself should have silenced the Doubting Thomas brigade, but of far more importance to me was the fact that I had not let Sheikh Saqr down and his trust in my youthful ability had been justified. I realised only too well that any expansion of the Mobile Force at this time was a non-starter financially or politically, and I had no wish to burden His Highness or the Crown Prince with any additional problems on their already burdened shoulders.

It had also been decided that Sheikh Sultan bin Saqr, the Ruler's second son, would be sent to England for officer training at Mons, and spend time in a military force on his return. I remember taking him to England and both of us were well aware of what was in store for him as he had spent time with me at the

Mobile Force prior to his departure. We had spoken at length about the physical and mental challenges he would have to overcome at Officer Cadet School and, knowing him as well as I did, I was confident he would achieve a first-class result. We went first to Moss Bros in Covent Garden to fit him out with some suits before delivering him to the strict military discipline that awaited him. Sultan was a most likeable, happy young man and everyone was delighted when he passed his officer training course with flying colours. A group of us from Ras Al Khaimah, including the Crown Prince, the Bevan family, Graham Barnett (who was about to join the TOS and is now chairman of the officers' branch of the TOS veterans) and me, were proudly present at his Passing Out Parade and able to congratulate him on his achievement. On his return, he spent time with the TOS but I realised that his future rightly belonged in Ras Al Khaimah with the Mobile Force.

We continued to concentrate on improving our military skills, and more and more I gave increased responsibility to my highly efficient and capable second-in-command, Major Mifta bin Abdulla Al Khatiri. I fully realised that by taking this action I could easily face making myself redundant but my only concern at the time, should this happen, was to leave the Mobile Force of which I was so proud in capable hands. The last thing I wanted was to stay on regardless when I had completed my objective, until eventually given my marching orders. On the other hand, there was no way I would contemplate any decision if it would add to the momentous problems Sheikh Saqr was facing on a daily basis. My loyalty to him and Ras Al Khaimah was total and unshakeable, which I am sure he knew and appreciated.

While all the frequent meetings were taking place to try and resolve the issues around the union and the Tunb islands, I would be discreetly asked by British officials from the Political Agency in Dubai for information. With the full knowledge and permission of Sheikh Saqr, I made it very clear to them that there was no hidden agenda and the simple truth was that the future of the Tunb islands was not negotiable, irrespective of any lucrative offer Iran might make.

The British government, while agreeing in principle that the islands belonged to Ras Al Khaimah, strongly urged that a deal be worked out for Iran to take possession of them. The explanation offered by HMG was that Ras Al Khaimah, despite the 'all-powerful Mobile Force' and the available police resources, was not in a position to provide an adequately powerful security force to control the entrance to the Strait of Hormuz from the Tunb islands. Iran had made it very clear that, once the British ceased to provide external protection to the region, it would not accept that the safety of the international shipping passing through the Straits should be in the hands of the new fledgling Union. Various proposals were put forward, such as a possible lease agreement and huge financial incentives, including the building of hospitals, schools and roads. These were all emphatically turned down by Sheikh Saqr, despite the British government pointing out that it would not be responsible for the security and protection of the region after 2 December 1971.

Almost up to the last day, HMG pleaded with Sheikh Saqr to agree a compromise deal, hinting that, if no peaceful solution were found, it could not be ruled out that Iran would take the military option and occupy the islands. Sheikh Saqr refused to compromise on his consistent stand, leaving the future of the islands to the will of Allah.

While the ongoing negotiations on the future of the Tunb islands were taking place, there had also been discussions between the Ruler, Trevor Bevan and me to strengthen the police presence on Greater Tunb. A decision had been made to place a detachment from the Mobile Force on the island, but the logistics to implement this still had to be worked out. As a first step, a new radio had already been installed to improve communications, with a link to our signal centre in the barracks and also to my house.

At dawn on 30 November, I was still in my house when I heard the operator on Greater Tunb trying to call me. We established contact and he quickly informed me that Iran was invading the island. He hurriedly explained that helicopters were flying around and it looked as if a ground force was about to land on the island as well. I was wide awake in seconds, but I could hardly believe what he was telling me. I was astonished by the news that Iran was launching an all-out attack on an island still under British protection. The operator remained incredibly calm and requested instructions on how to deal with this invasion. I told him the detachment were to take any action necessary to protect themselves and that I would report back once I had spoken to Sheikh Saqr.

I put the operator on standby, hurriedly dressed, drove to the Ruler's residence only a few minutes away and entered the courtyard. One of the Ruler's domestic staff appeared and I told him to call His Highness and that I needed to see him immediately. Sheikh Saqr appeared, greeted me in his usual friendly way and asked me what needed his attention so urgently at that early hour.

Once I had briefed him on the Iranian invasion with the sketchy information I had, his mood changed abruptly. He told me to assemble every dhow possible and be ready to sail with the Mobile Force and as many armed volunteers as we could muster. It was apparent that his initial intention was that we would all set off together to the rescue of the islands in our wooden dhows, defeat or put to flight the Iranian Navy, and recapture the islands.

This was not quite the reply I was anticipating. Bravery is one thing, but the thought of our wooden fleet challenging the strength of the Iranian Navy, which would be supported by helicopters, did not seem a very practical option – not to mention that the chances of emerging victorious from such a conflict were realistically zero. However, I dutifully replied to Sheikh Saqr that if those were His Highness's wishes then naturally they would be obeyed, and once our mighty 'armada' was in place we would set sail for Greater Tunb some 70 kilometres away. He then thought for a moment, and told me to wait while he prayed.

It was a moment in my life that I will never forget. The sun was beginning to rise and in the quiet dawn of a new day I stood watching the man for whom I had enormous respect, all on his own, praying. He had just given orders that would guarantee a watery grave for us all if we carried them out. However, our respect and affection for him was so great that, despite the certain fatal consequences of such an assault, I knew we would have no hesitation in sailing to the rescue of the islands. The thought went through my mind that I also should get down on my knees to repent of my past sins and promise to be a perfect Christian for the short remainder of my life. I realised, however, that there would not have been enough time to confess everything, so I just had to hope that 'He' was in a forgiving mood!

Sheikh Saqr finished his prayers, came back to me and calmly said that, following his meditation, he realised that he could not send his subjects on an impossible mission that could only end in death and defeat. We looked at each other knowing this was the only sensible decision, but I assured him that we were more than ready and willing to set sail for the islands if he requested it. Sheikh Saqr thanked me, but instructed me to radio the police section on the island and inform them that they were to lay down their weapons and surrender. He also told me to tell them that he would act swiftly to secure their release and to thank them for their bravery and loyalty. That very special moment in time comes back to me frequently and my close relationship with His Highness Sheikh Saqr, which had always been there, was strengthened even further on that fateful, historic morning.

I quickly returned to my house to carry out the Ruler's instructions, but discovered that there was no response to my urgent transmission to the island, at which point I assumed that the Iranians had already occupied the police base.

Hurriedly, I rejoined Sheikh Saqr to find out what our next move would be, and it was not long before the police and Mobile Force were on full alert, not sure what to expect next. The Iranians had surprised everyone and had carried out their illegal invasion and occupation of the Tunb islands while the Trucial States were still in theory entitled to protection by the British government against outside aggression, albeit there was only one day of that UK responsibility remaining. I have read many differing reports on what allegedly took place that fateful day, but in 2013 I was at last able to interview two of the policeman who were actually there and their descriptions of the events are very similar.

The six-strong police section, under the command of Lance Corporal Salem Suhail, was coming to the end of a two-month deployment on the island and was due to be relieved. One member of the section, Mohammed bin Abdulla bin Obaid, told me that they first sighted an Iranian ship approaching the island at about 5 am. Five helicopters then flew overhead, dropping leaflets with a message in Farsi. The leaflets advised the inhabitants and police not to fire or resist the Iranian troops and to surrender peacefully. A group of approximately 30 Iranian soldiers then landed and, in the gunfight that followed, the commander of the Iranian forces (later reported as being a close friend or relative of the Shah) was killed, together with eight (or nine) of his men. Lance Corporal Salem Suhail was fatally wounded while attempting to protect the Ras Al Khaimah flag, and four of the remaining policeman in the section were wounded, including Mohammed, who was shot in the leg. He proudly showed me the scar from that wound, which was still clearly visible.

The second policeman I was privileged to interview was Hamtoo Abdulla Mohammed, a Yemeni who has lived in the UAE since the incident. Hamtoo was the signaller on duty that morning and he recalls his efforts to make contact with the Ras Al Khaimah mainland to receive instructions following the invasion. It was a very emotional moment for both of us when he realised that I was the person to whom he had spoken. He remembered my initial instruction and that I would report back once I had spoken to Sheikh Saqr. After this he had left his radio to pass on my message, but never returned to it because they came under heavy fire from the Iranians and, despite their spirited defence, were overpowered and taken prisoner. After the invasion, the five surviving policemen were taken off the island by helicopter and flown to Iran. No consideration was given to the seriousness of their wounds or their general condition, and they were roughly handled by the Iranian soldiers. Hamtoo was the only policeman not wounded, and he was handcuffed and blindfolded and also removed from the island by helicopter once the others had already departed. The local Ras Al Khaimah fishing community of around 200 people who lived on the island were sent back to Ras Al Khaimah later in the day, having first hurriedly buried Lance Corporal Salem Suhail. His undoubted exceptional bravery has rightly been recognised and he has entered into the folklore and history of Ras Al Khaimah. The wounded policemen were initially taken to a hospital in Banda Langa in southern Iran, and were finally released some months later. They returned to a well-deserved heroes' welcome, attended by Sheikh Saqr and the entire Ras Al Khaimah population.

The invasion of the islands was promptly brought to the attention of the Political Agent in Dubai by the Crown Prince, who demanded immediate action. He further asked to be informed when the British forces would begin to evict the Iranians from the Tunb islands. I helped Sheikh Saqr and Sheikh Khalid with the wording of a telegram that the Ruler sent personally to the British Prime Minister, Edward Heath, demanding 'urgent action to be taken with a view to effecting the immediate withdrawal from the Islands'. He added that the 'outrageous Iranian attack was a breach of our treaty with the British Government, which is supposed to protect our people and soil against any foreign aggression'.

I phoned Peter Snow, the ITV reporter, asking him to ensure maximum coverage of the invasion and to put pressure on Whitehall, which seemed to have been caught with its pants down. The political response from the British government was as expected. They reminded Sheikh Saqr that they had repeatedly warned him that, unless he came to a compromise with Iran over the Tunb islands, military force by Iran could not be ruled out. They had also pleaded with him to come to a last-minute deal similar to the agreement reached between Sharjah and Iran over the future of Abu Musa, but he had refused. However, the British government did advise that, because the occupation had occurred before the formal handover from HMG to the proposed union, the UK would send a strongly worded letter of protest about the incident. This no doubt terrified the Iranians!

It is only now, with dusty archives revealing their previously hidden confidential material, that it is possible to learn more about what was going on behind the scenes. I had always been of the opinion that a secret agreement had been 'brokered' between the British and Iran over the future of the Tunb islands, but it would appear this was not the case. In June 1971, the Foreign Secretary, Sir Alec Douglas-Home, recommended to Prime Minister Edward Heath that the best policy was 'to keep the Iranians talking for the rest of the year and let the Shah seize the Islands by force, if he really is determined to do this, after the termination of our protection at the end of the year'. He continued that this would 'put most of the odium for an illegal act squarely on him'.

To add to the intrigue, Peter Ramsbotham, the British Ambassador to Iran, whom I met when he visited Sheikh Saqr to discuss the Tunb islands, wrote to the Foreign Office after a meeting with the Shah on 7 September 1971. He advised that the Shah had threatened to leave the Central Treaty Organisation unless the island dispute was resolved in his favour and that 'Iran would not tolerate a Union of Arab Sheikhdoms which could claim sovereignty over Iranian territory'. The Shah 'would at once oppose and destroy the Union and deploy all resources to that end'.

On 9 September 1971, Ramsbotham again wrote to the Foreign Office that a 'special relationship' between the UK and Iran would be proposed on a successful outcome regarding the disputed islands. This would include political cooperation in the Gulf and Indian Ocean, with increased orders for British weapons, contracts for British manufacturers and a moderate Iranian policy on oil matters. No wonder the British government was working overtime to achieve a settlement in Iran's favour. Interestingly, when speaking on 18 October 1985 to the Harvard University Center for Middle Eastern Studies, Peter Ramsbotham said he thought that turning a blind eye to the Iranian takeover was 'not a very proud moment for the British Empire, but it was the only way we could avoid a showdown'.

It is not known for certain, as far as I am aware, why Iran decided to take this military action when the Trucial States were still under British protection for only another couple of days. It was probably in the hope that public anger in the Gulf would be directed mainly against the British government for failing to comply with its treaty obligations and come to the rescue of the islands. If this was Iran's intention, it failed. There was a great deal of anger and resentment towards

Britain, but the focus of the rioting and looting that followed was concentrated on property, including banks and shops, with an Iranian connection.

The day following the Iranian invasion of the Tunb islands was my birthday, and it is certainly one for which I can still vividly remember my whereabouts.

The next couple of days were hectic. Naturally, both the RAKMF and the Ras Al Khaimah police did their best to maintain law and order, but it was a case of being able to provide only a very thin line of protection, and considerable damage was inflicted on Iranian-owned property.

On one occasion, we received information that a very large crowd had gathered in the old town and the situation was rapidly getting out of control. I happened to be with Sheikh Saqr when this news came through, and he immediately set off to see the situation for himself, accompanied by his usual Mobile Force escort. The Ruler told me that it would be unwise for me to accompany him, as anti-British feeling was also running high. This was totally unacceptable to me, as I wanted it to be clearly understood by everyone that I too was part of Ras Al Khaimah and I was not responsible for where I was born. Sheikh Saqr accepted this comment, which was from my heart, and I followed his vehicle, accompanied by my soldiers. When we arrived at the site of the demonstration, Sheikh Saqr got out of his vehicle to face an angry crowd of several thousand people who were demanding action as they marched towards us. The Ruler stood his ground, and looked directly at the crowd, who now became more subdued in his presence. Sheikh Saqr then called some of the ringleaders by name to come and talk with him. He patiently explained the situation and made it quite clear that, as the leaders of the demonstration, he held them responsible for ensuring it would be peaceful. The Ruler's discussion with them worked like a dream. There was a noticeable change in the mood of the crowd, from the previous threatening behaviour to a totally understandable demonstration of anger and frustration. It was an extraordinary example of Sheikh Saqr's influence and power over his people, which enabled him to achieve the result he desired purely by his presence and words. His method of confronting the crowd on that occasion was considerably more effective than any approach by a group of police or my own armed men would have been.

The British government's attitude and official response to Iran's invasion of the Tunb islands was an embarrassment to me and other British subjects. HMG was fully aware that Iran had invaded an island that belonged to Ras Al Khaimah, and which it was still legally obliged to protect, but it chose to ignore this obligation. Wringing their hands, rather like Pontius Pilate, the UK's political representatives were quick to remind us once again that we had been warned of the consequences of failing to come to terms with Iran and, regrettably, Ras Al Khaimah had suffered as a result.

Sometime after the invasion, Sheikh Saqr was interviewed about the events and, in response to a particular question, he said 'I considered sending an armed force back to Greater Tunb, to show our resistance. But the Iranians had the best armaments that money could buy and we only had rifles. The loss of one life, our policeman defending the initial attack, was already too high a price.'

Sheikh Saqr continued to keep the Tunb islands on the international political agenda and the UAE still makes regular mention of this act of aggression through the United Nations and other international bodies. Despite this, to date Iran has rejected any diplomatic moves to address the future of the islands.

By the end of 1971, it was obvious that the anticipated discovery of commercial quantities of oil in Ras Al Khaimah had not materialised and that the State would have to take the only practical remaining option, which was to join the union. Iran had illegally occupied the Tunb islands and there was no realistic chance of Ras Al Khaimah negotiating successfully with Iran on its own, whereas a much stronger challenge could be made from within the union. Anger at the Iranian invasion of the islands was felt throughout the Arab world; Iraq severed diplomatic relations with Britain, and Libya nationalised Britain's oil interests for what it considered Britain's complicity in Arab land being taken by Iran.

Just over a month after the Tunb islands invasion, I had reluctantly come to the conclusion that my time in Ras Al Khaimah was probably coming to an end. There was no practical requirement to increase the size of my Mobile Force, and neither was the necessary funding available even if such a requirement had existed. I was also satisfied that I had achieved all that had been asked of me. Major Mifta bin Abdulla al Khatiri, my very able and competent second-in-command, was more than capable of assuming command and, in time, consideration would have to be given to a command role for Sheikh Sultan bin Saqr.

I had not signed a contract stipulating the duration or terms and conditions of my appointment, as Sheikh Saqr and I had simply shaken hands to confirm the arrangements, which was all that had been necessary. It was unthinkable for me even to consider overstaying my welcome, knowing that I had completed my job, and I certainly did not wish to become an expensive and unnecessary embarrassment. Apart from that, I had no desire at all to become part of the Union Defence Force that was about to be formed. It was inevitable that, once Ras Al Khaimah formally joined the Union, the Mobile Force would, in time, be integrated into it. The thought of being a subordinate and on the receiving end of orders once again, did not appeal. However, I had never given any serious thought to 'life after Ras Al Khaimah'. I had naively presumed I would be there for the rest of my adult life and considered Ras Al Khaimah to be my permanent home.

Sadly, the decision about how and when to terminate my service in Ras Al Khaimah was eventually made for me. Sheikh Khalid, the Crown Prince, and I had, over the years, achieved an enormous amount together and also enjoyed a close friendship based on loyalty and trust. However, this relationship was shattered by a single incident and, although it was through no fault of my own and nothing to do with my military duties, I felt I had no option but to resign as I could no longer contemplate working closely with him. With the wisdom of hindsight, I now realise that I could have handled the situation differently, but at the time it was very clear to me that there was only one possible course of action – to resign and leave Ras Al Khaimah. I was not in a mood for compromise or to accept an apology from Sheikh Khalid himself, even if offered, and called on Sheikh Saqr the next morning to inform him of my decision to leave.

I explained to His Highness that my military task had been completed and that both Major Mifta bin Abdulla Al Khatiri and the Ruler's second son, Sultan bin Saqr, were more than capable and ready to take command of the Mobile Force before its inevitable amalgamation into the proposed Union Defence Force. I also made it very clear that I had no wish to be part of the UDF.

As always, Sheikh Saqr listened intently to what I had to say, but then he told me that the reason I had given him for leaving was not acceptable. He explained that I had left the British Army at his request and he realised that this had been a momentous decision for me. He added that, in asking me to take that action, he considered that my future would always be in Ras Al Khaimah. Sheikh Saqr also made it very clear that if, at some later stage, he decided to move me from the Mobile Force, another suitable position would be found.

He went on to say that, as far as he was concerned, I was a member of his family and, apart from offering me a salary increase, that was the end of the discussion.

This was an incredibly moving moment for me, and when I replied that, with a heavy heart, I had no option but to leave, he looked at me and asked if there was a problem between Sheikh Khalid and me? Once again, Sheikh Saqr demonstrated his amazing gift for reading between the lines, and I confirmed that he was correct, without elaborating further. Sheikh Saqr then reluctantly agreed that I would take a month or so away from Ras Al Khaimah, both to let the dust settle and to give me the opportunity to plan my future if I still decided to leave. I realised only too well that, although I was the innocent party, it would not be possible for me to remain and continue in Ras Al Khaimah as if nothing had happened. I therefore had no option but to do the honourable thing and fall on my sword. Gus and I packed up the various personal possessions that I had acquired over the years, including a collection of antique firearms, and put everything into storage until I had decided what to do next in my life.

I travelled to Beirut, a city I really enjoyed, and after a couple of days moved up to the beautiful Cedar Mountains for a skiing holiday. This had been arranged for me by my good friend Danny Chamoun, a frequent visitor to Ras Al Khaimah. His father, Camille, had been President of Lebanon and at that time Danny was an extremely popular leading political figure who many thought would follow in his father's footsteps. Some years later, I was deeply saddened to hear that he and his wife and their two sons had been brutally murdered in what was obviously a politically motivated assassination.

Apart from taking skiing lessons, which did little to improve my pathetic performance on the slopes, I visited the birthplace and grave of Khalil Gibran, author of the 1923 book, *The Prophet*. I spent several hours at his isolated grave, high up in the mountains, admiring the stunning views, reflecting on my life and wondering what the future had in store for me after Ras Al Khaimah.

My brother Roger, who by now was Head of Security for the United Nations in Geneva, came and joined me, which I much appreciated. The Neild brothers' skiing skills could not be described as particularly impressive, especially when we both managed to fall off a ski lift, fortunately before we had reached a dangerous height. However, we were probably in a class of our own when it came to the après-ski activity, and had a great time socialising with a lot of the Lebanese elite as well as enjoying the magnificent scenery and the wine to the full. Lebanon is such a beautiful country with so much to offer, and it is a tragedy that it suffers from so many problems that threaten to tear it apart.

Some totally unexpected news brought my relaxed vacation down to earth with a bump, but not in any way similar to those I had regularly been experiencing on the ski slopes. I received a telegram at my hotel informing me that the Ruler of Sharjah had just been assassinated and I was required to return to the UAE urgently. The telegram was signed by Sheikh Abdul Aziz bin Mohammed, a good friend of mine, and the brother of the Ruler who had just been murdered. Sheikh Abdul Aziz and I had served together in the TOS and he had been one the first Arab officers, together with Sheikh Faisal bin Sultan of Ras Al Khaimah, to pass out from the Mons Officer Cadet School. On his return he had served with distinction, and he was a popular and well-respected officer. The telegram went on to explain that Sheikh Abdul Aziz and the ruling family had consulted with Sheikh Saqr of Ras Al Khaimah following the tragedy and the latter had suggested that I should be contacted immediately.

Sharjah and Ras Al Khaimah have a common history, with both ruling families belonging to the Qawasim tribe, and it was therefore not out of the ordinary for the two families to consult each other at a time of crisis. Technically I was a free agent with no obligation to return, and I had already been considering the options for my future away from the Gulf. Having received this startling news, however, it took me only a few seconds to make my decision to book a seat on the next available plane to Dubai.

In 1965, some seven years before this crisis, the then Ruler of Sharjah, Sheikh Saqr bin Sultan, had been ousted in a bloodless coup and replaced by Sheikh Khalid bin Mohammed Al Qasimi. The events leading to the change of ruler at that time had undoubtedly been achieved mainly because Sheikh Saqr bin Sultan's political policies were more pro-Arab nationalism rather than Western.

In January 1972, only a month or so after the formation of the UAE, the deposed Ruler, Sheikh Saqr bin Sultan, must have considered that it would be an opportune time to reclaim his position and landed back in the UAE and assembled a small group of supporters. They attacked the Ruler's palace and shot dead Sheikh Khalid bin Mohammed Al Qasimi in his bedroom. As many as five others were killed and seven wounded. The rebels assumed power but their victory was short-lived as a strong force, comprising elements of the newly formed UDF and supported by additional forces from Abu Dhabi and Dubai, arrived to surround the palace. The rebels were quickly overpowered and Sheikh Saqr bin Sultan was arrested and shortly afterwards deported once again. Sheikh Saqr bin Mohammed, a member of the Sharjah ruling family, was appointed as the interim ruler until June 1972, when HH Dr Sultan bin Mohammed Al Qasimi (Khalid's brother) was elected as the new Ruler with the full support of the ruling family, as well as of the newly formed Federal Supreme Council of the UAE (made up of the Rulers of all the Emirates).

I did, however, learn later from reports now available in the British National Archives that, for some inexplicable reason, the Sharjah Police Commander at the time, Bob Burns, suggested to the Political Agent in Dubai that I should be questioned about the incident. However, this never happened and Bob and I became good friends.

What is abundantly clear is that the deposed Ruler presumed that he had sufficient popular local support, which would rally around him to return him to his previous position as Ruler of Sharjah. He also probably thought that because the Federal Supreme Council had only recently been formed it would not be in a position to take immediate, firm and decisive action. He was proved very wrong on both counts.

There was a considerable amount of correspondence within the British government in the aftermath of this failed attempted coup. On 25 January 1972, Miles Hudson, Political Secretary to Foreign Secretary Sir Alec Douglas-Home, wrote to Robert Andrew, Private Secretary to the Defence Secretary, stating:

> I have heard that Lord Carrington [Defence Secretary] is likely to come under attack at his meeting with the Conservative Defence and Foreign Affairs Committee on the grounds that the murder of the Ruler of Sharjah merely confirms what certain MPs have already said, namely that withdrawal from the Gulf would lead to instability, that had the British military presence not been withdrawn the attack would not have taken place and that our Gulf policy is in ruins. …

> Lord Carrington may like to see the attached defensive points produced by the Department here on this matter.

> (a) The Ruler of Sharjah's death is greatly to be regretted but unfortunately there has been a tradition of political assassinations in the area (three out of the last five Rulers of Abu Dhabi, for example, died violent deaths).

(b) The recent assassination was to a considerable degree a continuation of a family feud. The ex-Ruler of Sharjah, who staged the attempted coup, was himself deposed by his family in 1965 and has been trying to stir up trouble while in exile ever since.

(c) The presence of British troops did not prevent an assassination attempt on the Ruler of Sharjah last year when a bomb was placed under his chair. It was a lucky chance that by being late for his appointment he was not killed on that occasion.

(d) British troops in any case never had an internal security role and it would have been the Trucial Oman Scouts (now the Union Defence Force) which would have taken action.

(e) Unfortunately public personalities cannot be wholly protected from determined assailants who are prepared to ignore their own fate (cf. the ink throwing attack on the Prime Minister in Brussels).

I subsequently learned that my good friend Sheikh Abdul Aziz had been given the responsibility of restoring law and order in Sharjah and, with his excellent military background, he had the necessary experience to ensure the future safety of the Ruler and his family. Once in charge of security, Sheikh Abdul Aziz sent me the telegram asking me to return immediately to assist him in setting up a military force similar to the RAKMF. One moment, high up in the Cedar Mountains, I had been quietly reflecting on my recent decision to leave Ras Al Khaimah, and the next I was heading for Sharjah to start my second private army. Life can be very full of surprises!

BACK TO SHARJAH

My emotions were still flying high when the plane touched down at Dubai International Airport. During my month in Lebanon I had just about come to terms with my abrupt departure from Ras Al Khaimah and had been planning a new life away from the Gulf. Suddenly, I was returning to Sharjah to help an emirate that I presumed would still be in a state of disbelief and shock following the assassination of its ruler, and I questioned my ability to be of service at this tragic time.

On arrival, I was immediately taken to the Ruler's palace to meet Sheikh Abdul Aziz and other members of the ruling family. Understandably, he was not his normal, full-of-life self and I could see the sadness on the faces of all the others.

Sheikh Abdul Aziz told me that the decision had already been taken by the ruling family to establish immediately a military unit tasked to ensure the internal security of Sharjah and the protection of the Ruler and his close family. Funds were readily available for the establishment of this force, which was to be known as the Sharjah National Guard (SNG). Sheikh Abdul Aziz also confirmed that HH Sheikh Saqr bin Mohammed Al Qasimi, the Ruler of Ras al Khaimah, had recommended that I should be contacted and invited to return to assist them at this critical time. I was later told by Sheikh Abdul Aziz that Sheikh Saqr was extremely pleased that I had returned and wished me well.

Discussions then followed with the interim Ruler of Sharjah, Sheikh Saqr bin Mohammad, and Sheikh Abdul Aziz bin Mohammed to plan the creation of the

Sharjah National Guard as quickly as possible. I informed them that I was happy to assist in the formation of the new local force but had no wish to remain once I considered it to be operational. This was accepted, and they decided that I would be in command of the force with Sheikh Abdul Aziz as my 2i/c. I was offered and accepted the same rank and similar personal terms and conditions to those I had received in the RAKMF, and then it was time to get 'boots on the ground'.

It was only after that first meeting that the reality of the situation began to sink in. Only one month after considering my military career was at an end. I was I back in uniform and about to form and command my second independent army. The Trucial Oman Scouts had now become the Union Defence Force, but other emirates still maintained their own independent armies. It would be many years before most of them felt sufficiently secure to allow their own forces to merge into one combined, powerful army.

There was an uneasy calm in Sharjah at this time as the people came to terms with the tragic events and mourned the assassination of their popular and respected ruler. It is true that there had been a history of coups in many of the old States, but a deposed ruler returning after seven years in overseas exile and attempting to seize power by force was hard for all Emiratis to take in.

Shortly after my return to Sharjah, there were developments back in Ras Al Khaimah. Following the recent Iranian invasion of the Tunb islands and the assassination in Sharjah, Sheikh Saqr held lengthy discussions with his family and other Ras Al Khaimah dignitaries, and it was agreed that Ras Al Khaimah would join the Union.

We immediately started recruiting for the Sharjah National Guard, and the UDF allowed soldiers from Sharjah to transfer to their new home force (as had the TOS when the RAKMF was established). This was much appreciated, and enabled us to have trained soldiers patrolling the town to reassure the Sharjah residents that law and order had been restored and that normal daily life was possible once more.

In a relatively short time, with Sheikh Abdul Aziz as my competent second-in-command, we had managed to recruit mainly experienced, well-trained soldiers who were soon wearing our newly designed uniforms and armed with the same conventional weapons being used by the other forces in the region. The majority of our purchases were again made through the Crown Agents, who provided, as they had done in Ras Al Khaimah, an efficient and speedy service.

It was comparatively straightforward the second time around, since I knew who to contact and where to look for some of our requirements. In addition, there was no need to design and locate new barracks, as we were able to take over buildings that had been part of the old TOS Sharjah camp, which had been put at our disposal. I even had my own Officers' Mess with an abundance of efficient, friendly staff to take care of me, but it was a bit lonely since Sheikh Abdul Aziz, the only other officer at the time, normally went home each night. Gus happily took control of everything and I have a suspicion that one of his self-appointed duties was to sample all the meals that the superb cook prepared for me, as his waistline expanded significantly once we moved into the Mess.

I quickly devoted my time and efforts to my new task and was pleased with the steady progress that was being achieved. There was still the odd unfavourable comment made about me by some officers now serving in the UDF, who had only recently been posted to the Gulf and who had never even served with me. I suppose that human behaviour of this nature was to be expected considering my position and age, but it still annoyed me, especially as I already had a successful proven military record in Ras Al Khaimah.

The only matter of real importance to me was the fact that not just one, but now two rulers had sufficient faith and trust in my ability to bring peace and stability to their respective States. This was the highest compliment possible and there was no way I would ever let them down.

My earlier military experience in Ras Al Khaimah was now proving to be very beneficial in organising the establishment of the SNG, and with Sheikh Abdul Aziz as my dependable anchor we were well pleased with our early results. Within a few months we were able to present a reasonably well-trained company of well over 100 men. It also helped enormously that my 2i/c was the brother of the newly appointed Ruler of Sharjah. (In June 1972, the ruling family united behind HH Dr Sultan bin Mohammed Al Qasimi, who had previously been appointed the first Minister of Education of the new Union in December 1971.) Sheikh Abdul Aziz was able to resolve many potential delicate issues in no time at all. Sadly, he died from cancer in 2004, but I am sure that if he were still around he would agree with me that we made a formidable professional team.

In approximately six months the SNG was operational and had taken full responsibility for the security of the Ruler and his family, and we were competent to respond to any civil unrest or other emergency. I continued to concentrate most of my efforts more on the logistical requirements and ensuring the training programme covered all contingencies which the fledgling force might have to encounter. However, the first test of our readiness to handle any emergency took us all by surprise and was certainly not one for which we had trained.

On 14 March 1972, we received reports that radio contact had been lost with a commercial airliner that was due to land for refuelling in Dubai. Sadly, it soon became clear that Sterling Airways flight 296, a Sud Aviation Caravelle, must have come down somewhere en route to Dubai and we eventually heard that an explosion had been reported in the mountain range near Kalba, an area belonging to Sharjah.

Helicopters found the wreckage at first light the next morning, but the crash site covered a large expanse in the mountainous region some 1,600 feet above sea level, which was virtually impossible to reach other than by helicopter. It was also tragically clear that there was no hope of finding any of the 112 passengers and crew alive. I will never forget the scene of total carnage that I witnessed on my first flight over the area, but nothing could prepare me for the appalling scene on the ground. Air disaster experts, together with senior personnel from the airline, arrived in Sharjah very rapidly to supervise the salvage operation and a hotel on the outskirts of Sharjah city was taken over to accommodate all of us involved in the operation. A control room was set up to coordinate the recovery of the bodies and I committed the SNG to carry out this gruesome but necessary task.

It was quite bizarre to observe businessmen from companies specialising in services for natural and manmade disasters arrive unannounced to see what business (and profit) they could make. One company that I remember particularly well was represented by two London brothers, who appeared at the control centre offering to sell lined coffins. They assured me these would be needed because wooden ones would not be suitable. Once the operation to recover what was left of the passengers and crew was under way, we quickly realised that they were absolutely right and a sealed coffin to prevent leakage of body fluids was absolutely essential. An order was immediately placed with their company and the necessary lined coffins were air-freighted out from their UK warehouse the same day. Gruesome as it may sound, the 'coffin company' actually provided an essential service which solved one huge and sensitive problem.

Unless one has been personally involved in a disaster of this magnitude, it is impossible to begin to comprehend the wide range of supporting resources required to deal with the emergency in a professional way. Experienced rescue experts arrived and I accompanied the first team by helicopter to inspect the situation on the ground. Before preparing to leave, I was surprised when they advised me not to use any normal soap or aftershave. They explained that the smell of these familiar products in the future would bring back memories of what we were about to experience. Taking their advice, I used a tin of oriental balm one of them had given to me, which I applied liberally to my top lip to try, not very successfully, to lessen the impact of the dreadful smell at the crash site.

The plane had flown straight into the mountain ridge, which meant that, fortunately, the passengers would have had no warning of the impending crash. One moment they would have probably been relaxing with a drink in their hand, reminiscing about their recent holiday, and the next moment oblivion, or whatever else happens when we die. We never found one body intact – only various parts, not remotely recognisable as male or female, adult or child.

One of the many lessons I learned from this disaster was the distressing personal consequences of such accidents. No settlement of estate or insurance could be made for years unless a passenger was positively identified. The fact that a missing person's name was listed as a passenger was not acceptable in a court of law as sufficient proof that the person was physically on the plane. For these reasons, it was stressed to all involved in the recovery operation that it was vital to recover as many remnants as possible, in the hope that the forensic team would be able to match something identifiable and make a positive identity. The huge cold storage depot at the old Sharjah barracks became a temporary morgue, where these highly dedicated officials carried out their inspections and investigations, albeit often with a bottle of beer in one hand. They were totally committed to finding and examining any personal effects or any other distinguishing feature that would provide acceptable confirmation of the identity of a person – a necessity, in order to spare a loved one from having to wait years to finalise the legalities. My soldiers and I spent four days wearing protective clothing in the intensely uncomfortable and worsening conditions at the extensive crash site, where we went the extra mile to ensure we recovered as many of the scattered human parts as possible and placed them in plastic bags for transfer by helicopter to the waiting forensic staff.

Each night, exhausted both emotionally and physically, I would step into the shower in my hotel room, having first removed the soiled clothing and slugged down a large amount of whisky straight from the bottle. This was in the futile hope that, while the shower cleansed the outer body, the 'Scottish medicinal treatment' would help wash away the terrible sights we had observed and the memory of the morbid manual tasks we had had to carry out. It was a dreadful experience but, once again, my Arab soldiers proved their resilience, which made me incredibly proud of them. It was also reassuring to know that our actions had enabled many of the victims to be identified so that their heart-broken relatives were able to mourn their loved ones.

It had become abundantly clear from my initial discussions that the decision to form the SNG had understandably been taken on the rebound following the assassination of the Ruler. It was also obvious to me that this new local force would inevitably, at a later stage, be integrated into the UDF, together with the RAKMF and other independent emirate forces. Since I had no wish to be involved in the UDF, I knew I would not stay in the region much longer.

I spent the next 12 months ensuring that the SNG was capable and equipped to provide the security for the ruling family and trained to react efficiently and effectively to any internal situation in the emirate in the unlikely event of any unrest. We now had a force of over 300 men and, once their training was completed to my personal satisfaction, I knew it was the correct time to pack up and put soldiering, and the Gulf, behind me.

I requested an audience with the Ruler to inform him of my decision, though I realised he would have been aware my plans to leave as I had already discussed them with his brother, my second-in-command and good friend Sheikh Abdul Aziz. His Highness kindly asked me to reconsider and to stay longer, but I knew it was the right decision and time to move on. In the back of my mind I have often wondered whether the Ruler was concerned about his brother, Sheikh Abdul Aziz, taking command of the SNG. It is now a matter of history that, while the Ruler was out of the country in 1987, his brother did stage a coup, but it lasted just over a week before it was put down and Sheikh Abdul Aziz was banished from Sharjah.

During my time in the Gulf, I witnessed the beginning of the incredible transformation that has been achieved from the vast wealth generated from oil. I had been fortunate to serve with the TOS on two secondments and also formed and commanded the independent armies for Ras Al Khaimah and Sharjah, both of which I was immensely proud. I knew that I would be leaving with a heavy heart and that it would be painful to say farewell for the last time to so many friends, especially my devoted faithful shadow Gus, who had been with me for all my service in the Gulf going back to 1959. I made sure that I provided him with more than sufficient financial support to enable him to enjoy his life and choose his own future without ever having to find another job. Much later, I discovered that Gus had been tempted to invest his money in the lucrative local gold trade, but he had drowned attempting to bring a heavy load of bullion ashore from a dhow. He could not swim, which made this terrible tragedy even harder for me to bear. Never a day goes by without my thinking of him. Rest in peace, old friend.

Although I had given up a permanent career in the British Army and the associated pension, I had managed to save a reasonable nest egg, which was beginning to burn a big hole in my bachelor pocket. It was now time to find pastures new, spend some of my funds wisely on wine, women and song, and blow the balance on the non-essentials of life!

LIFE AFTER THE GULF

I was fortunate that, on leaving the Gulf, I had many options to consider. Two decisions that I had already made were that I would not live permanently in England and that I would somehow put my influential Arab contacts to good use. At the age of 35, I was still relatively young and a bachelor, and had sufficient funds to allow me to travel at will for a considerable time before I needed to put down permanent roots anywhere. I decided to return to Kenya, where I had served with the King's Regiment, and spent nearly two years training to be a professional hunter. It was my intention, once qualified, to bring Arab clients on hunting safaris, as many of my old friends had expressed a keen interest in coming to hunt big game in Africa. The Kenyan government banned hunting shortly before I was ready to set up my own safari company, but I was actually pleased about this as I much preferred 'shooting' those magnificent animals with a camera.

From Kenya I moved down to South Africa, but it took only a short while under the apartheid regime there to realise that it was not for me. I took the advice of Peter Maxwell, an old friend in the entertainment business, who was in Johannesburg at the time, and headed for Rhodesia.

From the moment I walked into the Long Bar in Meikles Hotel, Salisbury, in 1973, I knew that I had found what I was looking for. I could not fault the description 'God's Own Country'. Not only did I fall in love with the country, but I also met and fell in love with Eileen, who became my wife. I became a tobacco farmer on our beautiful Wengi Farm, but I soon spent more time away from the farm as an active member of an eight-man police reserve stick made up from fellow farmers. They were all great characters and were very much at home in the bush, and we spent the next few years together heavily involved in fighting the terrorist insurgency.

Very unexpectedly, in 1982 I mysteriously received an invitation to visit Malawi with all costs paid, an offer my curiosity would not allow me to turn down. It was the start of a journey that lasted for the next 13 incredible years. I became the General Manager of the Chamwavi Group, an agricultural organisation that was privately owned by the Life President of Malawi, Dr Hastings Kamuzu Banda. I soon learned, to my horror, that no one had lasted for more than one year in this sensitive position, but His Excellency, as he was always referred to, and I built up a sound working relationship. Much to the amazement of many, including local politicians, this association lasted until 1995, when he lost his title of 'Life President' in elections held at the insistence of the Western world. Eileen, our daughter Michelle and I look back on those years in the 'Warm Heart of Africa' with great nostalgia, especially Michelle as she met and married her wonderful husband Sean there.

We then settled in post-apartheid South Africa in the picturesque town of George (named after the British monarch George III), situated at the heart of the beautiful Garden Route, where we had already purchased our home several years earlier. Somehow, Eileen had also managed to get the previous owner to rent his former property from us for all the years until we finally took up residence ourselves – an incredible deal by an incredible woman!

Much to our delight, a few years later Sean and Michelle and our granddaughters Samantha and Kimberly also made the move from Malawi. George has an abundance of top-rate golf courses that I enjoyed playing, including the one and only George Golf Club. Only a short distance away is the internationally renowned Fancourt Golf Resort, venue of the Presidents Cup in 2003, and where I had the honour to serve as Captain for two years. It was also where I met and became good friends with Ernie Els and his family. To this day, fellow golfers who have had the misfortune to play with me and observe my 'unique' swing refuse to believe that on one occasion I actually beat Ernie. The fact that I had introduced him to port (my favourite tipple) the previous night of course had nothing to do with this epic victory – though Ernie may not agree!

I had lost contact with all my TOS colleagues during my travels but once settled in South Africa this was rectified. Two separate TOS branches for ex-officers and NCOs had been established and I started to receive regular newsletters from my old friend Leslie Barron informing us all of the activities and whereabouts of the 'old and bold' and sadly, all too frequently, to tell us of those veterans who had moved on to the final desert oasis. I was particularly sad to learn that Desmond Cosgrove and Ken Wilson were no longer around and had departed this life far too early. They had both been very special friends, and it was Desmond who had made it possible for me to join the King's Regiment.

In 2002, a TOS reunion was arranged thanks mainly to the efforts of David Sievwright, who served with the TOS after my time, and Tim Courtenay, an ex-Royal Marine who I knew well. This was a wonderful opportunity for all those interested and still capable of making the journey to return to the Gulf to meet up with old Arab colleagues and friends, and witness at first hand the transformation that was taking place. This reunion was held courtesy of the UAE Ministry of Defence and I was delighted to sign up for the trip and eagerly looked forward to it.

I flew in from South Africa and met up with the UK contingent at the splendid UAE Officers' Club in Abu Dhabi. Once we had all finally recognised each other and come to terms with our distinguished elderly appearances, the party was on.

The main topic of conversation initially focused on our various knee and hip replacements and prostate problems, but in time we began to reminisce about the time we had all served together and our discussion turned to the 'do you remember' theme. Our very full itinerary, which included visiting old campsites in various emirates, enabled us to meet up with many of the old Arab veterans.

The reception we received wherever we went was absolutely incredible and I am certain that it was the first time that any of us old veterans realised the significance of our role all those years before, enabling the peaceful formation of the United Arab Emirates.

On this first reunion, we attended a Passing Out parade for newly commissioned officers at Al Ain and we were all most impressed by the high standards we witnessed. HH Sheikh Khalifa bin Zayed Al Nahyan, Crown Prince of Abu Dhabi, addressed the young officers on parade. He singled out three reasons for the smooth transition from the seven independent states into the harmony that is enjoyed in the United Arab Emirates today. The first was the will of Almighty Allah, the second was the wisdom and vision of his father,

Sheikh Zayed, and the third, he said, pointing in our direction, was 'those old gentlemen sitting over there'. There was a huge roar of agreement from all present, which certainly sent a tingle up and down my spine and no doubt did the same for everyone else in our reunion party.

On a personal note, that first reunion enabled me to meet up with many of my old military friends including Rashid bin Abdullah (my Sergeant Major at the arrest of Saif bin Ali), Abdullah Ali Al Kaabi (now a retired major general with whom I had served and since become close friends), and our first Arab TOS commissioned officers, Sheikh Abdul Aziz bin Mohammed and Sheikh Faisal bin Sultan. This, I was discreetly told later, was the first time that Sheikh Abdul Aziz had been allowed back into Sharjah territory since his attempted coup in June 1987. Permission had been granted for him to attend a reception in our honour at a Sharjah hotel owned by Sheikh Faisal bin Sultan. Sadly, Sheikh Abdul Aziz died two years later after a long battle against cancer. During his time in a London hospital he received frequent visits from old TOS friends, which he told me he really appreciated.

Also included in our itinerary was a visit to Ras Al Khaimah to meet up with HH Sheikh Saqr. I presumed that Sheikh Khalid, the Crown Prince, would be in attendance and I wondered what type of reception I would receive from him. On arrival at the palace in Ras Al Khaimah, we were informed that the Crown Prince was unfortunately out of the country, but his brother Sheikh Sultan bin Saqr would be present with his father.

Much to our surprise and delight, an announcement was made at the start of the reception that we were all to receive the Ras Al Khaimah Order of the Qawasim. This, we were told, was in recognition of and gratitude for the vital role that the TOS had played in creating and maintaining the peaceful environment which made the United Arab Emirates possible. This was a truly great honour, and I know that all of us fortunate to have been there that day now wear that medal with special pride. We visited most of the emirates on that first reunion, but it was worthy of note that Ras Al Khaimah, which in the past had sometimes unfairly been criticised for not being fully supportive of the TOS role in the old Trucial States, was the only emirate to bestow such a prestigious order of merit on those of us attending the reunion.

When it was my turn to step forward and receive my award from Sheikh Saqr, he repeated my name several times and then asked if it really was me. His Highness was now an old man and his sight had deteriorated, so he needed confirmation that it was me standing in front of him. I happily announced that I was overjoyed to be once more in his presence after all those years. Then, in front of the large gathering assembled to observe the awards ceremony, we embraced and hugged each other, and I was very close to tears. It was a most moving moment, but fortunately Sheikh Saqr's second son, Sheikh Sultan, who was standing next to us, intervened and, with his well-known sense of humour, quickly restored the happiness of the occasion. I spent some time after the reception with Sheikh Saqr and Sheikh Sultan, and they both made me promise that I would return again soon.

In 2003, the year after my first visit back to Ras Al Khaimah, Sheikh Khalid was replaced as Crown Prince by his brother, Sheikh Saud, and Sheikh Khalid left the emirate. This announcement came as a complete shock to me but, realistically, it also meant that it would be much easier for me to keep my promise and return to Ras Al Khaimah on a more regular basis in the future.

Eileen accompanied me on two further trips and was at last able to meet not only Sheikh Saqr, but also many of my other old Arab friends about whom she had heard me talk so much. This meant a great deal to me, and it was quickly apparent that she shared my affection for the people and the region. I had known the new Crown Prince, Sheikh Saud, since he was a young teenager, when he would occasionally visit the Mobile Force barracks with his cousin Sheikh Ahmed bin Humaid, who was a serving officer. He took a keen interest in the military at that time and I remember we had a uniform made for him in the hope that it might influence him to consider a military future. It is unquestionably for the best that our plan did not succeed, since he has been free to devote his remarkable talents and energy to transforming the emirate into what it has become today.

It was on our second visit, in 2008, that Eileen and I saw Sheikh Saqr for what turned out to be the last time. His Highness had returned to spend most of his time at the old fort where he had lived in his early days and, as was his custom, he sat outside each day with his faithful armed retainers reminiscing about the old days. It was here that Eileen and I found him and sat with him for over an hour. We did not speak much, but words were not necessary to express our special relationship or the many memories we shared. It was fitting that, in his final days, he wanted to be close again to the peaceful surroundings of the fort which, like him, had witnessed so much of the history of Ras Al Khaimah. When it was time to take our leave I knew, sadly only too well, that it would be for the last time. Holding his hand, I managed to utter a few tearful words and saluted him, and, with a heavy heart, we left.

In 2010, Eileen and I decided that the time had come to consider the possibility of leaving South Africa and finally returning to the country of our birth, England. It was not an easy decision to make and we agreed to get a feel for living out of Africa by first moving to Cyprus as a halfway stopover. We explained to our confused and bewildered family and friends that the 'logic' for selecting Cyprus as a stepping stone to England was that, as British passport holders, we would have no problem taking up residence there since Cyprus was by now part of the European Union and they drove on the left. If things did not work out, we still had our family and home in George to return to.

The second TOS reunion in the UAE took place in 2012 while we were still enjoying our Mediterranean lifestyle and, once again, David Sievwright and Tim Courtenay were the highly efficient organisers. Somehow, with remarkable composure, they managed to get all us old-timers in the right place at the right time – no easy task. The warmth of our reception wherever we went was as overwhelming as the previous time, ten years earlier, and one could not help but marvel at the changes and development that had taken place. It was on this trip that I first met HH Sheikh Saud as the Ruler of Ras Al Khaimah, following the death of his father in 2010. I had watched the events related to Sheikh Saqr's passing on Abu Dhabi Television, which fortunately we could receive in Cyprus. Realising it was the end of an era, I felt desperately sad and wanted so badly to be there with the huge gathering of mourners from all over the UAE and beyond to pay my respects to his family that I had been privileged to know. The emirates, and Ras Al Khaimah in particular, had lost a most respected dedicated and visionary leader and I had lost the man who had made such an impact on my life and who I looked up to as a father. He is always in my thoughts and I am so grateful that he played such an important role in my life. May his soul rest in peace.

There was no time during the 2012 TOS reunion reception in Ras Al Khaimah to have a private conversation with HH Sheikh Saud, but the following day he kindly sent a car for me. I was collected from our Dubai hotel by Khalil, a highly competent and friendly palace driver, who was able to bring me up to date with much of the Ras Al Khaimah news. Sheikh Saud and I had a most enjoyable lunch together and at some point Sheikh Saud proposed that he would like me to write a book about my personal early memories, not only in Ras Al Khaimah but of all my time in the Gulf. I was happy to agree and, on my return to Cyprus, where Eileen and I had then been living for two years, I started to put pen to paper (or, more correctly, finger to keyboard).

In February 2013, Sheikh Saud generously invited family members of those of us who had worked in Ras Al Khaimah in the early days, before the birth of the UAE, to return for a visit as his guests. Merilyn Bevan (daughter of Trevor, the police commander) and her son Simon, Margaret McKay (widow of Bob from the Agricultural Research Farm at Dig Dagga), and daughter Fiona, Ruth Ash ('Miriam', Angel of the Desert) and niece Catherine, plus Eileen and I made up the 'old-timers' group. 'Jundee' Sanderson, who had coordinated the UK travel arrangements, and Hugh Nicklin as photographer (both ex-Trucial Oman Scouts) completed our group along with my good friend Dr Saif Baddawi, an active historian on all TOS matters. We enjoyed a fascinating itinerary, organised by the Ras Al Khaimah Government Protocol Office. We were also fortunate to have the services of Geoff Pitts, Deputy Director General for Customs Operations in Ras Al Khaimah, to look after us. Geoff had 'volunteered' for this task and, with his attention to detail and efficient manner, he managed to take personal care of us all, which was much appreciated. I would have no hesitation in giving him an excellent reference should he ever decide to switch career and become a travel guide!

Undoubtedly, Ruth/'Miriam' was deservedly the star of the show, which came as no surprise. She had cared for so many of the local population during her time in Ras Al Khaimah that many of them, or perhaps their parents, had her to thank for surviving those harsh times when there was very little in the way of hospitals or even clinics. One very memorable day of our tour was spent high up in the mountains with the tribesmen. It was a huge celebration with much dancing and feasting that none of us who were privileged to be present will ever forget. Once again, we experienced the genuine gratitude the people felt towards us for the part we had played in the development of Ras Al Khaimah. It was a most moving and humbling experience.

The day before our departure, I had a final meeting with HH Sheikh Saud to report on the progress of my book and he kindly said that I was welcome to return to Ras Al Khaimah at any time to carry out further research, which was a wonderful gesture.

As agreed, I duly returned to Ras Al Khaimah some two months later to carry out some research for the book. It then came as a wonderful surprise when His Highness told me that he wanted Eileen and me to come and live permanently in Ras Al Khaimah. As always Eileen, on hearing this incredible news, was totally supportive, and she was as excited as I was to accept this generous invitation, which would enable us to reside again in the one place that had always remained so special to me. I felt that at last I was coming home.

RAS AL KHAIMAH
THEN AND NOW

The Ras Al Khaimah that Eileen and I have the good fortune to witness and experience on a daily basis has changed dramatically from the small town I knew and loved all those years ago. Magnificent hotels and villas have replaced the coastline *barasti* dwellings but family, tribal customs and tradition remain and manage to coexist in harmony with the hustle and bustle of modern-day life. This is quite remarkable considering the visible changes that have occurred with the vast wealth that oil has brought to the region. Back in my early military days, the Trucial States were incredibly poor and the people survived in harsh, basic conditions similar to their ancestors. Friendships that I and others made with our Arab colleagues then were genuine and had nothing to do with wealth, as none of us had any! Many of my old Arab friends have sadly passed on, but their sons and relatives still remember me and wherever I go I continue to be very moved by the incredible warmth of their greeting.

Since my return in 2013, I have had time to reflect on those early days and make comparisons with the Ras Al Khaimah of today, which makes me shake my head in wonder and disbelief.

From the original, humble quarry mine whose operations were frequently interrupted by rifle fire from the mountain tribesman, two hugely successful quarry companies have developed and are now recognised as being among the leading quarry operations in the world.

I think back to the late 1960s and recall how excited we all were when the British Bank of the Middle East (since absorbed into HSBC) opened a branch in Ras Al Khaimah. Although it was just a small concern then, with only a few staff, we could cash a cheque in Ras Al Khaimah for the first time, albeit only after lengthy bureaucratic procedures and careful scrutiny of one's account. RAKBANK (National Bank of Ras Al Khaimah) was founded in 1976, and today is one of the leading and fastest-growing banks in the UAE. I don't think the bank staff in that lone BBME branch would have coped too well with the huge number of customers that use RAKBANK today.

Back in those early days in Ras Al Khaimah, we few expat residents would sometimes search the shoreline in the hope of finding 'treasure' washed ashore from sunken ships. Local history records that numerous galleons had been wrecked in the area, and occasionally the sea gave up some of their precious cargo. Sadly, I was never lucky enough to come across any gold or jewellery during any of my many hours of searching, but this does not surprise me; I have great difficulty even in finding my golf balls, which are regularly attracted to the most remote areas of courses. However, we did come across numerous fragments of blue-and-white Ming china.

Today the emirate is the proud home of the Ras Al Khaimah Ceramics Company, which is the world's largest producer of ceramics and exports goods all over the world, including to China. Not once, while searching the seashore and picking up pieces of china on those beautiful unspoiled beaches and sand dunes five decades ago, did we imagine that Ras Al Khaimah would one day be home to the world's leading ceramic manufacturer.

When I first came to the Gulf, in 1959, the vast majority of local inhabitants were illiterate as there were very few schools or other places of learning available to provide education. Sheikh Saqr and his son Sheikh Saud have always considered the provision of education for their subjects to be a key priority. Mainly due to the collapse of the pearl-diving industry in the 1930s, only limited income was available to the rulers to invest in education.

Soon after becoming Ruler in 1948, Sheikh Saqr, aided by funding from Kuwait, started a boy's school for 34 students, who were housed in tents near his fort. In 1956, he started the first girl's school in the Trucial States. Sheikh Saqr also introduced for the first time a 'school police policy', which penalised parents if they did not ensure that their children attended school!

These basic but important first steps formed the foundation for Ras Al Khaimah's current growth and are reflected in the ongoing priority given to education in the emirate. Ras Al Khaimah now hosts a variety of places of learning, including international schools and universities. HH Sheikh Saud has stated that 'We recognise that we in Ras Al Khaimah are only as good as the schools we have and without good schools we cannot realise our dreams or take hold of our future'.

When I pass the numerous medical facilities and hospitals now available in Ras Al Khaimah, I always think of Ruth (or 'Miriam') starting out with those few syringe needles that she had to sharpen with emery paper. There are now a number of government hospitals available to all residents, including the Saqr Hospital in Ras Al Khaimah city and the new Sheikh Khalifa Specialist Hospital, built on a main road into the city, which provides highly sophisticated medical treatment.

With the increased prosperity in the region, many people have taken the opportunity to obtain private health insurance for their families. Several private hospitals are available, including the Swiss-managed Ras Al Khaimah Hospital with its team of highly professional and friendly staff. Both Eileen and I have used this hospital for routine check-ups and have enjoyed the excellent care and the comforting reassurance that we have not yet reached our shelf-life expiry date.

Fortunately, after a visit to the doctor most of us only need a bit of fine-tuning, with a lecture encouraging us to improve our lifestyle and a prescription for some pills. I am sure that Ruth and I never envisaged the day that Ras Al Khaimah would be home to one of the biggest pharmaceutical companies in the world, producing a wide variety of medications. During our pioneering days in the emirate, very few doctors were available to prescribe any pills that were needed and it was another challenge to find a pharmacy. Even then, there was no guarantee that the medication you required would be available.

Julphar (Gulf Pharmaceutical Industries) was established in 1980 when Sheikh Saqr was still the Ruler. It is now the largest pharmaceuticals company in the region, producing well over 180 brands of mainly generic, high-tech drugs.

In 1969, I had to travel to London to purchase Ferret armoured cars for the RAKMF, but today I would need to go no further than the Ras Al Khaimah Free Trade Zone to do my shopping. There are now over 8,000 companies from 100 countries operating in the RAKFTZ and two of these companies specialise in the production of armoured cars and VIP protection in luxury cars.

In the late 1960s, the handful of lucky expatriates living in Ras Al Khaimah shared the magnificent natural scenic beauty with the local population, who numbered around 25,000. Even then, we realised that this quiet, serene environment could not last forever and that it was only a matter of time before others discovered our closely guarded secret. The Ras Al Khaimah Hotel, built on a high point offering stunning sea and mountain views, was the first commercial tourist hotel to open at that time, and thus began the Ras Al Khaimah tourism industry. Although the majority of the hotel's guests came initially in the holiday seasons and at weekends, there was a steady stream of businessmen keen to explore the potential for trade. This changed dramatically, however, when, to everyone's surprise, a casino was allowed to open in the hotel. This unexpected and controversial development attracted a different type of customer, and brought not only curious gamblers to try their luck on the wheel of fortune but also some shady individuals. Most of the seven Trucial States still had little income at that time and relied on a number of initiatives to generate much-needed funds, such as the issue of colourful commemorative stamps and even their own coins. The casino, however, was not well received by the local people of the Trucial States, and not simply because gambling was only permitted for non-citizens. It not only raised many eyebrows, but also lowered my bank account balance because, for some inexplicable reason, my 'foolproof winning roulette system' was no match for the croupiers. The population in general (and my bank manager in particular) were very relieved when the decision was taken after only a few months to close the casino down. The hotel could then once again concentrate on attracting tourists to discover the many charms of Ras Al Khaimah that we had selfishly tried to keep to ourselves.

Ever since the birth of the United Arab Emirates in December 1971, the 'prophets of doom' have predicted that the new country would not survive in its present form, and in the aftermath of the recent Arab Spring these predictions have arisen once again. Changes will most certainly continue to take place in the region, but only at the rate dictated by the wishes of the rulers and their people.

I am very confident that Ras Al Khaimah will continue to develop in a steady and responsible manner, committed as a part of the United Arab Emirates, under the far-sighted, proven leadership of HH Sheikh Saud bin Saqr Al Qasimi. He will ensure that the vision for the development of Ras Al Khaimah that was started by his father, HH Sheikh Saqr bin Mohammed Al Qasimi, will continue to go from strength to strength for the benefit of all.

For my part, it is a dream come true to live in Ras Al Khaimah once again and to have Eileen to share the dream with me. She has already been captivated by all she has seen, and shares my love of the people and everything associated with Ras Al Khaimah.

The memories of those early, special Ras Al Khaimah days and the people of all races and religions that I was privileged to know and serve with remain constantly in my thoughts. I consider myself most fortunate to have worked closely and been guided by HH Sheikh Saqr bin Mohammed Al Qasimi and to have observed at first hand his wise counsel and to witness his profound contribution to the successful, peaceful transition to the United Arab Emirates. It is also a source of great pride for me that the sons of those great early leaders have built on the solid foundations they inherited and continue to develop a country that has emerged from its desert past to become united, peaceful and well respected throughout the world.

The momentous development that has already been achieved in my lifetime is quite remarkable, and Eileen and I look forward to following the progress that continues to be made at a breathtaking pace. I have no doubt that this will continue for generations to come, and nowhere will it be more apparent than in the unique and unforgettable emirate of Ras Al Khaimah.

ACKNOWLEDGEMENTS

I have dreamed for years of recording the incredible and often vivid memories of the years that I spent in the Trucial States, and at long last this ambition has been realised. This would never have materialised without the generous encouragement and support of HH Sheikh Saud bin Saqr Al Qasimi, the present Ruler of Ras Al Khaimah, who clearly has a passionate desire to establish a true record of historical events relating to the emirate and its people. His untiring enthusiasm to secure historical information about the development of Ras Al Khaimah has most certainly been a major influence in my decision finally to write about my times in the Gulf. Eileen and I will be eternally grateful to him for his continued kindness, which is very special and means so much to us.

I have also learned that the art of soldiering and that of a would-be author are very different, and I most certainly would not have been able to attempt the challenge without the encouragement and unwavering support of my wonderful wife, Eileen. How she continues to put up with me after nearly 40 years is a mystery, but long may it continue. Not only has she been a loving mother and wife, but she is also my closest friend and soulmate.

I am also extremely grateful to my good friend, Geoff Pitts, who 'volunteered' to read and review my early manuscripts while they were being written. His constructive comments and suggestions have been of immense importance and he has been a great source of support. Eileen and I miss him enormously now that he has left Ras Al Khaimah after five years of loyal and dedicated service with the Customs Department. We hope that he will enjoy his retirement in Southampton with his lovely wife Deborah.

Huge thanks are also due to Dr Ash Rossiter. This book has benefited enormously from his research, including the additional information he gathered from the British National Archives relating to the historical and political background to so many key events relevant to the history of Ras Al Khaimah. A special thank you also to Hannah Rossiter for taking the excellent photographs of HH Sheikh Saud bin Saqr Al Qasimi and myself at the Ruler's Palace. Ash, Hannah, their young son Samuel and the latest family addition, Freddie Saif, who was born here in Ras Al Khaimah in 2014, not forgetting the good dog Logan, have become close friends and we enjoyed the good times spent with them in Ras Al Khaimah. I wish Ash well in his new position at the Khalifa University in Abu Dhabi.

I am extremely grateful to Bill Cruikshank, Jon Cousins and Ruth Ash for allowing me to include some of their personal memories, which have added so much to this book. I am also indebted to my old friend Sheikh Faisal bin Sultan Al Qasimi for putting his vast collection of photographs at my disposal.

My thanks are due to Dr Natasha Ridge and Jessica Andrews of the Sheikh Saud bin Saqr Al Qasimi Foundation for Policy Research in Ras Al Khaimah, who have provided assistance and encouragement in the review of my manuscript; their advice and suggestions have been very helpful.

I am extremely grateful to Dr Nigel Rea, Advisor at the Ras Al Khaimah Palace. With his eye for detail and knowledge of the UAE, Nigel has helped me enormously to turn the early draft into the book that is now finally ready for publication. At all times he delivered his constructive comments to me with a smile, even when pointing out some of my more basic errors. Nigel has had to burn the midnight oil to find time in his busy working schedule to take on my book and I sincerely appreciate his dedicated input.

It was only towards the final edit of this book that a publisher was selected. My thanks are due to Steven Rice, who introduced me to Roger Harrison, non-executive Director of Medina Publishing, over lunch at the Al Hamra Golf Club. Medina Publishing specialises mainly in books related to the Middle East and is now setting up an office in Ras Al Khaimah. Both Roger Harrison, based here in Ras Al Khaimah, and Kitty Carruthers (founding Director) in England have given me tremendous support and encouragement.

Despite all the assistance and support I have received to ensure that this is an accurate record of events from my time in the Gulf, I take full responsibility for any inaccuracies, factual or stylistic, that may have occurred due to an unreliable old memory.

It is my sincere wish that this book will bring back memories to some and help others to have a better understanding of the fascinating history and remarkable development of this truly amazing country.

David Neild, Ras Al Khaimah, July 2015.

BIBLIOGRAPHY

British Policy in the Persian Gulf 1961–1968: Conceptions of Informal Empire. Helene von Bismarck, Palgrave Macmillan. 2013.

Two Alpha Lima: The First Ten Years of the Trucial Oman Levies and Trucial Oman Scouts (1950 to 1960). Peter Clayton. Janus Publishing Co. 1994.

Arabian Days: The Memoirs of Two Trucial Oman Scouts. Antony Cawston and Michael Curtis. Michael Curtis. 2010.

Saqr. Fifty Years and More. Graeme H Wilson. Media Prima. 2007.

The Parting Years: A British Family and the End of Empire. Sheila Bevan. Radcliffe Press. 2001.

The Trucial States. Donald Hawley. George Allen and Unwin Ltd. 1970.

The Emirates: Witness to a Metamorphosis. Donald Hawley. Michael Russell (Publishing) Ltd. 2007.

PICTURE CREDITS

All pictures from the author's collection except the following, for which the author expresses gratitude:

front cover: Captain Ian Stewart, 2ic B Squadron, Trucial Oman Scouts
back cover: David Parker
pp. 4 & 6: Hannah Rossiter

Plate section:

p.i: Jashanmals
p. v (top & bottom) Sheikh Faisal bin Sultan Al Qasimi
p. vi (top) David Parker, (bottom) Ruth Willis
p.vii (top & bottom) British Library
p.vii (top) Merilyn Anderson
p.ix Ras Al Khaimah Museum
pp.xi, xii National Archives Abu Dhabi
p.xvi Andrew Godber

INDEX